FIGHT LIKE A TIGER

FIGHT

LIKE A

TIGER

Conway Barbour and the Challenges
of the Black Middle Class
in Nineteenth-Century America

VICTORIA L. HARRISON

Southern Illinois University Press
Carbondale

Southern Illinois University Press
www.siupress.com

Portions of the author's article "Man in the Middle: Conway Barbour and
the Free Black Experience in Antebellum Louisville," *Ohio Valley History*
10, no. 4 (Winter 2010), 25–45, appear in this book with permission from
the Filson Historical Society. Portions of the author's article "We Are
Here Assembled: Illinois Colored Conventions, 1853–1873," *Journal of the
Illinois State Historical Society* 108, nos. 3–4 (Fall/Winter 2015), 322–46,
appear in this book courtesy of the University of Illinois Press.

21 20 19 18   4 3 2 1

Cover illustration: Samuel Harrison

Library of Congress Cataloging-in-Publication Data
Names: Harrison, Victoria L., author.
Title: Fight like a tiger : Conway Barbour and the challenges of the black
   middle class in nineteenth-century America / Victoria L. Harrison.
Description: Carbondale, IL : Southern Illinois University Press, [2018] |
   Includes bibliographical references and index.
Identifiers: LCCN 2018003036 | ISBN 9780809336777 (pbk. : alk. paper) |
   ISBN 9780809336784 (e-book)
Subjects: LCSH: Barbour, Conway, –1876. | Middle class African
   Americans—Arkansas—History—19th century. | Middle class African
   Americans—Illinois—History—19th century. | Middle class African
   Americans—Kentucky—History—19th century. | Middle class African
   Americans—Ohio—History—19th century.
Classification: LCC E185 .H315 2018 | DDC 305.896/0730904—dc23 LC
   record available at https://lccn.loc.gov/2018003036

For Dave and Sam

Contents

Gallery of illustrations beginning on page 61

Acknowledgments

MANY PEOPLE HAVE helped with this project, but my greatest debt is to Silvana Siddali. Her generous guidance, insightful criticism, and encouragement have been invaluable to me over these many years. She is a brilliant scholar and the best editor I have ever known. Silvana understood what I was trying to do before I did and lit the path for me. She is a dear friend to whom I will be forever grateful. Shirley Portwood, a friend and mentor for more than thirty years, trained me and shaped my approach to historical inquiry. Her critiques are always both sharp and warm. I was proud to be R. Bentley Anderson's first graduate student. Mark Hull advised me even while at war. All improved this book immensely.

As I worked and reworked the book, I benefited from Silvana's writing circle at Saint Louis University. Christopher Schnell, Stephen Kissell, and Eric Sears made helpful comments on each chapter. They are supportive friends and colleagues who made taking criticism easier than it might have been. And then there are the pastries!

I am indebted to innumerable librarians and archivists in the several states covered by Barbour's story, but I am particularly fond of Deirdre Johnson and Sara Miller, my interlibrary loan goddesses at Southern Illinois University Edwardsville. I would also like to thank my colleagues in the Department of Historical Studies who offered words of encouragement, especially Carole Frick, Bryan Jack, and Jessica Harris.

Thank you to Tom Dillard, Pen Bogert, Glenn Crothers, Dave Joens, and Elaine Evans. An earlier version of the first chapter was published in *Ohio Valley History*, and I am grateful to Lee Ann Whites and Craig Buthod of the Filson Historical Society for permission to republish that material. Some sections of chapters 2 and 3 appear courtesy of the University of Illinois Press. Sylvia Frank Rodrigue of Southern Illinois University Press has been a kind and reassuring presence in this process, and I thank her. Her colleague Judy Verdich is a pleasure to work with, as are Wayne Larsen and Robert M. Brown Jr. This project was supported by the College of Arts and Sciences, the Graduate School, and the Department of Historical Studies at Southern Illinois University Edwardsville.

My friends and family have lived with Conway Barbour for as long as I have, and I am very thankful for their patience and support. Thank you to Terri Costley, Denise Harrison, Debra Homyer, and especially my best friend, soul sister, and role model, Jeanette Howell. I cherish my brothers, Mark and John Whitehead, and sorely miss our parents and youngest sibling, Bill. Above all, thank you to my husband, Dave, and son, Sam. I have found no photos of Conway Barbour, but Sam created one using images of James Barbour and Conway's grandson, Thomas Conway Rankin. I am so proud of this talented young man. Both he and my husband of thirty-six years fill my life with laughter and my heart with joy. With great love, this book is for them.

FIGHT LIKE A TIGER

Introduction

ON THE AFTERNOON of 27 May 1871, Conway Barbour's home in Alton, Illinois, was auctioned and sold outside city hall. Purchased for $1,200 cash in 1864 and shelter to his wife and children, the homestead had served as collateral in many of Barbour's business ventures over the years. Now, the last of those businesses had failed, leaving the once-popular African American caterer and restaurateur with a mechanic's lien and order for sale from the chancery court.[1]

Barbour himself was probably not present for the auction. Facing debt and failure, he had long since turned in a new direction. Like other men trying to gain entry into the middle class, Barbour seized new opportunities where he found them. By the time the auction took place, Barbour had completed a term in the Arkansas legislature and was defending his appointment to a county office in the southeastern corner of the state. He was a typical nineteenth-century "man on the make," although his path was complicated by the color of his skin.

Stuart Blumin has argued that America's white middle class developed in the three decades before the Civil War as economic, social, and cultural transformations converged to create new habits of mind and self-identification. Melanie Archer and Judith Blau called attention to the importance of institution building, geographic mobility, and consumerism in constructing the middle class, as well as notions of civility and polite society. Richard Bushman described the material process in *The Refinement of America*; Karen Halttunen focused on the changing notions of acceptable behavior. While historians tend to emphasize certain aspects of what it meant to be middle class—wealth, work, possessions, demeanor, associations, self-conceit—there is general agreement about its development by the middle decades of the nineteenth century.[2]

The degree to which African Americans were a part of this shift is murkier. Because the vast majority of blacks were enslaved before the

Civil War and because free blacks were unwelcome in both North and South, some historians date the black middle class much later, retarded by the weight of American institutions. William Julius Wilson argued that although a small number of elite, propertied free blacks existed in the antebellum years, the development of the black middle class "accompanied the change from a preindustrial to an industrial system of production" that occurred in the late nineteenth century. Scholar Karyn Lacy puts it even later. In the ante- and immediately postbellum periods, she suggests, mulattos made elite by their white bloodline and lighter skin constituted a class separate from "darker" blacks. Their rank had nothing to do with income, occupation, or educational attainment but rested solely on their white ancestry. This applied to enslaved and free alike. Not until after World War I would a new group of middle-class blacks emerge, one whose educational attainment and refinement set them apart.[3]

Other scholars assert that the black middle class, although small, developed alongside Blumin's white middle class. Bushman found a small but identifiable black middle class in the early decades of the nineteenth century. Erica Ball has argued that black middle-class values are apparent in early-century print culture ranging from convention proceedings to slave narratives and black newspapers. I agree with this interpretation. I believe that African Americans shared the middle-class mores of the larger white society and did so at the same time, although this was made more difficult by a hostile environment and tumultuous national politics.[4]

Lacy's study of middle-class blacks in modern-day Washington, DC, describes variability across contexts of constructed social identities. Confronting racial discrimination even as they "make it," these middle-class families employ, among other devices, a "tool kit" of identities to distinguish themselves from middle-class whites, other middle-class blacks, and lower-class blacks. Strategically assimilating even as they value their unique "blackness," African Americans in Lacy's study find ways to negotiate the intersection of race and class in twenty-first-century America.

I would like to appropriate and adapt Lacy's notion of a tool kit for an aspiring black middle class in the nineteenth century. Because of the barriers to economic and social participation built into American society, African Americans who sought to enter the middle class negotiated tough terrain with both natural and acquired tools. These might include "accident of birth" attributes like mixed blood and innate intelligence; "environmental" tools such as exposure to contemporary notions of refinement and education/skills; and "personal competence" tools: the ability to ingratiate oneself with potential benefactors, the resourcefulness to identify and seize on opportunities as they appeared, and a willingness to bend the rules when necessary. Most important, perhaps, is a self-conceit that presumed inclusion even as it recognized the vulnerability of African Americans in white society, both before and after the Civil War. Not everyone aspiring to the middle class had all these tools at their disposal, and not everyone who had them was assured success. Some combination of these tools, however, strategically employed, was necessary for those wanting to move up in the world.

Conway Barbour was aspiring and had tools in all three categories. He was born a mulatto slave of the white Barbours, a wealthy and well-connected family that included federal officeholders and judges. Manumitted by his owner by early adulthood, Conway Barbour benefited from his mixed race. Mulattos received a lot of attention and commentary in the years before the Civil War. Critics of slavery pointed to them as evidence of sexual misbehavior by white owners, prompting some slavery advocates to defend that behavior—bizarrely—as beneficial to preserving the virtue of white women. Both sides, however, considered mulattos to be superior to darker men and women because of their white blood and thus gave them special treatment. This bias meant that mulattos were more likely to be emancipated, educated, and allowed to acquire skills. In Kentucky, for example, in 1860, 38 percent of free blacks were of mixed race compared with about 19 percent of slaves. By late in the antebellum period, the same white blood stirred fears of rebelliousness, leading proslavery forces to develop pseudoscientific reasons why the color line had to be hardened, but by then, Barbour was long free.[5]

His other "accident of birth" characteristic was intelligence. While it is unlikely he received any formal education, his ability to teach himself is evident, for example, in the letters he wrote in the early 1860s compared with those he penned a decade later. The earlier letters are full of spelling and grammatical errors, whereas those written in the 1870s to a Little Rock newspaper, a paper that disliked him and would have relished, not corrected, his mistakes, are much improved. As he was in his forties, with a growing family and businesses to run during the intervening years, his learning must have been autodidactic or assisted by his children. His natural abilities made this self-improvement possible.

Barbour's occupational skill set also served him well. In 1840s Louisville, he worked as a steamboat steward, a position offering good pay and a look at the outside world. The vast majority of free blacks in the

South lived in rural areas as farmers or casual laborers with little chance of bettering themselves. Urban environments, especially those on water like Louisville, offered more diversity of opportunity. By 1860, about a third of the South's free blacks lived in its cities. Many worked as teamsters, domestics, factory workers, and day laborers, for example, at the bottom of the economy, but some worked as barbers, carpenters, tailors, and other skilled artisans and businessmen. The kinds of jobs available to them varied over time and space as legal and customary restrictions were honored, ignored, or changed under pressure from white workingmen. The most common forbidden occupations involved sales of liquor or groceries, the presumption being that alcohol would produce rebelliousness and that opportunities to sell produce would encourage slaves to steal. Enforcement, however, was haphazard; many blacks owned grocery stores that doubled as bars. Employers sometimes preferred free blacks to white laborers because they were cheaper and could not testify against their bosses in court, disadvantages that African Americans turned to their advantage, even managing to monopolize some occupations. In certain trades where their labor was vital, such as caulking at shipyards, free blacks formed workingmen's associations to defend themselves against white competition. Opportunities for skilled work and a comfortable living were best for free blacks in the Lower South and diminished as one moved farther north. Ira Berlin has suggested this is because Lower South masters were more likely to provide their "selectively" freed individual slaves with skills and support, while Upper South masters, inspired by the American Revolution, gave freedom but nothing more.[6]

Barbour's experience is at odds with this generalization, as he acquired skills and a measure of financial security as a steward in Louisville. He also gained a familiarity with the finer things in life as a crewman on some of the most luxurious steamboats of the era. The authority vested in his position and the expertise he accumulated during those years fueled his ambition and raised his expectations for the future. When he advertised his restaurants in later years, he emphasized his background in managing the posh dining rooms of the finest riverboats. It was a point of personal pride.

In addition to natural and environmental tools, Barbour had a personal competence that allowed to him to recognize opportunities and pursue them. He made strategic alliances with prominent steamboat captains, civil rights advocates, financiers, and politicians. Over two decades in the middle of the century, he re-created himself again and again in pursuit of both material success and notoriety. His ambitions were sometimes thwarted by his race; sometimes, propelled; and most of the time he understood which was which and responded accordingly. His adventures give us some insight into the ways and means by which middle-class and would-be middle-class blacks pursued their goals in both the South and North as the country transitioned through its bloody Civil War and beyond.

Between 1855 and 1871, Barbour moved five times, and in each case he thought he saw better days over the horizon. In his willingness to chase chance, Barbour was like many Americans of his time, a people on the move. As an African American, he had to weigh his desire for improvement against what was possible in any specific location for a person of color. He had to filter place through race, but if he had any hesitations, they were overcome by his faith in himself and in his country.

Barbour was an optimist. Born a slave himself and then living among slaves in Louisville, he witnessed the cruelties of the institution and the indignities visited upon people who looked like him. And yet he never lost heart or his vision. He briefly toyed with the notion of emigration but then offered to participate in the defense of the nation, confident of his place in it. Steeped in what Gunnar Myrdal, another optimist, called the "American Creed," Barbour's idealism, like Myrdal's, was largely misplaced. The obstacles were many. Even so, an increasing number of African Americans, like Barbour, absorbed the same values as their white friends and fought for elevation, respectability, and even refinement.[7]

Conway Barbour was a relentless self-promoter who, as one contemporary said, knew well the value of printer's ink. His name appeared often in the press, especially in Alton and during his years in Arkansas. An ambitious man of talent and energy, Barbour reached out for opportunities whenever and wherever if they offered a chance to improve his reputation and bank account. His business dealings are virtually indecipherable as he manipulated property in four states to support his large family and his own ambitions. His occasional duplicity in both personal and public affairs is unlovely but not uncommon for businessmen and politicians then and now. It is this scheming and striving that places him fully within the broader culture of mid-nineteenth-century America. Sometimes he succeeded and more often he failed, but he never stopped trying. Barbour's desire and willingness to seek the main chance and to do what was necessary to obtain it represent the values of his time.

And he was not alone. In each place he lived, a small black middle class made up of skilled laborers and craftsmen, ministers, teachers, and entrepreneurs, among other occupations, valued home, family, education, and respectability. They participated in politics, churches, and civic organizations and set the standards for their communities. Their progress was complicated by slavery and racism, making their tool kits vitally important. Because of the structural barriers to their success, they were not always as well situated as their white counterparts. For historians, the definition of what constituted middle class cannot be exactly the same for white and black people in nineteenth-century America, despite similar values. Further, the difference between "elite" and "aspiring" African Americans can be difficult to characterize. Frederick Douglass was elite. Did a Chicago barber become so by his attendance at Douglass's Rochester convention? Or was he already elite as a small businessman?

Many black writers struggled to define class lines among African Americans. Cyprian Clamorgan, a member of St. Louis's "colored aristocracy," emphasized wealth as the primary differentiator between elites and the remainder of the black community, but he also considered deportment, skin color, and other factors. Philadelphia's Joseph Willson thought simply living comfortably in one's own home made one "higher class." Louisville's William Gibson described rivermen who achieved that independence as being "prominent." William Simmons's 177 *Men of Mark* were chosen for their stature as lawyers, politicians, preachers, educators, and writers, many with careers that did not make them rich. All were aspiring; some were elitists. But as August Meier wrote, elitism is in the nature of leadership, differentiating strivers from their neighbors in any case.[8]

That no one knows about Conway Barbour is the point. To say there was no black middle class before the late century is only to say we have not identified it beyond a rather narrow group of familiar writers. Part of the problem is the lack of sources. Barbour's life can be reconstructed in bits and pieces because he *did* like printer's ink, but there is no cache of papers to examine. The other problem is that we have convinced ourselves that slavery and racism were just too much for all except a very few African Americans to overcome, and so we have not gone looking for other men and women who did just that, who used their tool kits to make their way through and over obstacles and toward success as they defined it. I will argue that Barbour was one of many blacks who fought to better themselves alongside their white countrymen in the middle decades of the nineteenth century and passed down to their children a middle-class ethos far sooner than some historians have suggested.

Lexington and Louisville

PHILBERT AND MARY Jane Ratel taught music and dance in Lexington, Kentucky, in the 1820s. Although culturally elite, they were not wealthy: after Philbert died in early 1830, his probate inventory revealed that the Ratels had few belongings. They owned a piano, an old violin and a clarinet, a "small lot of French books," a carpet, a looking glass, a few items of furniture, and some teaspoons. None of it was worth very much. Aside from the couple's cash, $1,100 before expenses, their most valuable possession was their mulatto slave, Cornelia Bateman. All told, the estate, cash, and sundries were worth a little more than $1,400, and under Kentucky law, two-thirds of that belonged to their eleven-year-old son, William. Perhaps this is why Mary Jane reminded the *Kentucky Reporter* in February 1831 that she continued to give piano lessons at a friend's home at Second and Market or at her own residence near Medical Hall. Cornelia's future and the circumstances of her enslavement depended on the boy.[1]

Despite its cultural achievements, Lexington had a sinister side, the inevitable result of the institution of slavery. In Cheapside, between Main and Short Streets, slave men, women, and children were auctioned off to settle the estates of their owners, to raise money to clear debts, or simply to sell as merchandise. The offices, showrooms, and slave jails of the traders were nearby. Trader William Pullum's filthy slave pens were located behind the home of Mary Todd's grandmother on West Short Street; trader Lewis C. Robards's offices were across the street. The sights and smells of the slave trade were everywhere. Worse yet were the sounds, the screams of those tied to a tall, thick rod of locust wood in the northeast corner of the public square. Slaves who violated the rules were often punished at this whipping post.[2]

In the year before Ratel died, the slavery issue had become a source of great turmoil in Lexington. A proposal to ban the importation of slaves into Kentucky for the purpose of sale was before the state legislature.

Lexington's proslavery senator Robert Wickliffe condemned the bill; the city's prominent emancipationist Robert J. Breckinridge condemned Wickliffe. In early 1829, Charles Wickliffe, the senator's son, had murdered the editor of the pro-emancipationist *Kentucky Gazette* after the paper responded to an attack penned by young Wickliffe in the proslavery *Kentucky Reporter.* A sympathetic jury acquitted Charles, who then challenged the *Gazette*'s new editor, a boyhood friend, who criticized the jury's decision. Charles died in a duel with the man in October. As it would for many years to come, slavery was setting neighbor against neighbor in Lexington, turning friends into mortal enemies.[3]

The crisis escalated in 1831—shortly after the Turner rebellion in Virginia—when some slaveholders met in Lexington and formed a group promising to manumit the future children of their slaves at age twenty-one. Proslavery forces became hysterical and worked out their paranoia on the city's blacks. Slaves were suddenly charged with capital crimes ranging from burglary to murder, and although no slave had been executed in the county for more than a decade, four were hanged on a single day that August. The Nonimportation Act was finally approved in 1833, but by then, Lexingtonians had other things to worry about.[4]

Cholera brought unimaginable sorrow to Lexington in 1833, killing perhaps fifty people a day. From June 1 to August 1, more than five hundred people died. About half of Lexington's residents left the city, and those who stayed avoided each other for fear of contracting the disease. Commerce ceased. A shortage of doctors, coffins, and gravediggers meant that bodies were abandoned outside graveyards. Robert Todd donated trunks from his attic to those in Cheapside who were unable to get coffins. So many children were orphaned that the community collected a purse of $4,400 to fund an asylum for their shelter. Among the dead were free black tailor Edward Bateman and two of his children, Cornelia's family. And she was not alone. By one account, a family of nineteen lost seventeen people that summer.[5]

Mary Jane and William survived the epidemic and remained in Lexington until midcentury. William, now also a music professor, moved to Louisville about 1840. There, "Billy" Ratel became the highly esteemed leader of the city's Philharmonic Society and a prolific composer. With the help of his uncle, Theophile Aristide Vatble, a French émigré and Louisville importer, he also sold cigars and liquor. Mary Jane remained in Lexington until at least 1850, after which she too relocated to Louisville to teach music.[6]

Neither William nor Mary Jane seem to have been interested in keeping the slave Cornelia. By law, William owned two-thirds of the girl and so controlled her fate. Born only a few years apart, the two had grown up together through the 1820s and suffered together through Philbert's death in 1830. They were friends. Years later, William rented a fourteen-year-old slave girl to help his wife, Emily, tend to their son. Billy Ratel apparently had no problem with the institution of slavery. Such was his personal relationship with Cornelia, however, that she was functionally free by the early 1840s.[7]

Although sometimes witness to the worse excesses of slavery in Lexington, Cornelia had a personal experience of slavery different from that of many others in bondage, reminding us of the complexities of the institution. Instructors of music and dance, the Ratels aspired to a refinement that was unlikely to include harsh unpleasantness or corporal punishment. Philbert was praised in print for his "taste and judgment"; their advertisements in the *Kentucky Gazette* were for ladies and gentlemen interested in "fashionable" dancing. Although we can never know exactly how the Ratels treated Cornelia, it appears that she was allowed to pursue her own interests. In fact, by the early 1840s, she was married.[8]

On some unrecorded date, probably in Louisville, Cornelia Bateman became Cornelia Barbour, wife of Conway Barbour. Whereas she had grown up around cultured artists of modest means, Conway took his name from a prominent family of Virginia. Compared to many other black southerners, the couple was fortunate, and this forever shaped their expectations for what they might achieve and where they belonged in American society. By chance of birth and upbringing, they had the tools to seek what most of their white neighbors were seeking and most of their black neighbors could not: entry into the middle class.

The Virginia Barbours were a distinguished family in the Early Republic. James Barbour, a Scottish merchant, immigrated to Virginia before 1707, the year he married Elizabeth Taliaferro in what became Orange County. Their only son, also James, bought and sold real estate and fathered a large family by two sisters, Elizabeth and Sarah Todd, before his death in 1775. One of his many sons, Thomas Barbour, was a member of the Virginia House of Burgesses and an active patriot in the era of the revolution. He also presided over a large household that included another James, later governor of Virginia, a U.S. senator, secretary of war, and minister to England, and Philip Pendleton Barbour, a member of the U.S. House of Representatives and an associate justice of the U.S. Supreme Court. The family counted among its friends and associates Jefferson, Madison, John Taylor of Caroline, and many other luminaries of the founding decades.[9]

Thomas Barbour's sons and their many cousins accumulated land in both Virginia and Kentucky. By 1820, the extended family held acreage in Orange, Culpeper, Campbell, and Loudoun Counties in the Old Dominion as well as property in Washington, Jefferson, Mercer, and other counties in Kentucky. They were politicians, lawyers, planters, and the owners of other human beings. The fourth U.S. census found that three Barbours in Orange County—James, Philip Pendleton, and their brother, Thomas— owned a total of 188 slaves. The same census enumerated thirteen Barbour households in Kentucky—also including James, Philip Pendleton, and Thomas—with a total of 142 slaves and 11 "other" people neither white nor enslaved, that is, free people of color or Native Americans.[10]

The dearth of vital records for African Americans in the Early Republic often compels historians to reconstruct their lives from bits and frag- ments. This research entails both art and science, faith and skepticism. I am convinced that one of these slaves or other people was Conway Barbour, a mulatto born between 1815 and 1820 in Virginia. Barbour was born a slave and emancipated before the 1840s, although no writ of man- umission has been located. His obituary notice in the 1870s referred to him as having been "formerly a favorite servant of the governor," a ref- erence to James Barbour. The governor's biographer believes a paternal relationship would have been out of keeping with James's character, but at least one report suggests that James Barbour fathered a mulatto daughter in Richmond around the same time that Conway was born. James Bar- bour might have been Conway's father, uncle, or grandfather, but the two were connected. If Conway is taken at his word—and he must have given the information to the newspaper at some point in the early 1870s—the governor was his father, although Conway's name does not appear in the governor's papers. The exact nature of Conway Barbour's blood relation- ship to James Barbour is less important than his identification with the governor and its implications for his self-conceit.[11]

James Barbour, like so many men of his station, criticized slavery in theory while it made him rich in fact. Although he *said* the institution was as harmful to whites as to blacks, he took no steps to do anything about it. Instead, he accumulated human beings, the first in 1795. By the turn of the century, he owned ten slaves; by 1810, he owned forty-six, including fourteen children. Throughout most of his life, he typically owned more than a hundred slaves. And like most planters, Barbour kept detailed lists of and valuations for his "people." His 1817 "List of Negros belong to JB" included 110 slaves whose value he estimated at almost $50,000. The register was adjusted after the deaths of Sam ($500) and Cato ($750) and the births of Tabby's twins in 1818 and Fanny's Ruben in 1819, among others. A new list compiled in 1824 included the ages of all 121 people on the plantation. The organization of the list suggests that Barbour's first concern was the production of more slaves, not the formation of families. The register has the names of slave women followed by the names of their children. Men and women without children were listed at the end.[12]

In his public pronouncements, Barbour was an advocate of firm but generous treatment of slaves, reflecting the paternalism common to pro-slavery rhetoric. Speaking in 1825 before the Agricultural Society of Albemarle, a group he helped found, Barbour argued that treating slaves well was in planters' self-interest because healthy slaves worked harder. "Proper authority" over them, however, was essential. Owners who, out of a misguided sense of "humanity," did not make slaves work hard would see "speedy ruin." Slaves should be given bread without limit; a daily allowance of meat, milk, or cider according to the season; small amounts of whisky on proper occasions; three suits of clothes a year; and someone to cook and wash for them. He said he also gave rewards to the most deserving. His approach, he said, resulted in the slaves' gratitude and good conduct.[13]

Barbour's self-image required that his methods result in grateful, happy slaves, and the proof of his goodwill resided in his ledgers. Barbour kept close account of what was given to his people and by whom. In November 1833, some of his slaves received shoes. Sam, Major, Henry, and a couple others received their shoe allotment from Charles, possibly the "manager" who worked for Barbour for more than three decades. Barbour personally distributed shoes to other men and women on the plantation. He knew who got new socks and blankets and what he paid for weaving the slaves' cloth and buying their eggs. Barbour's version of benevolent despotism was in part an exercise in accounting.[14]

Like most slave owners, he had no use for free blacks. In the Albemarle speech, Barbour said free blacks were typically criminals: "to be rid of them is an object of our first desire." A dangerous example to those who were enslaved, free blacks threatened the world the masters made.

The rules could be different, however, when the person of color was your own flesh and blood. Martin Van Buren's vice president, Richard M. Johnson, scandalized Lexington society by his common-law marriage with his slave Julia Chinn. She was an octoroon and very light skinned; their two daughters were even lighter. Johnson was genuinely fond of all three women, educated his girls, and ignored the criticism heaped upon the whole family by its indignant neighbors. Arkansas planter Elisha Worthington's wife divorced him because his relationship with a slave produced two children, James W. and Martha Mason. The children lived in the house with their father except for when he sent them to Oberlin for schooling. One Mississippi planter, unable to bear the idea of his mulatto daughter living among slaves, sent her to Cleveland, where she lived in privilege with her own household staff. These examples suggest that slave owners sometimes valued their own blood more than racial custom. James Barbour's comments on the wretchedness of free blacks, then, may not necessarily have applied to members of his own family, including Conway Barbour, a free man by the 1840s.[15]

Although Cornelia was practically free, she was not legally free, and that was a problem. Because slavery followed the mother, she needed proof of emancipation before she and Conway started a family. William Ratel eased the way by putting his Uncle Vatble in charge of the matter, and so it was the Frenchman who freed her in Jefferson County court—twice—despite never actually owning her. Cornelia's first emancipation, in October 1842, referred to her by her married name, misspelled as Cornelia "Barber." The second emancipation, recorded three months later, was necessary because the first had excluded the required wording about a bond and because Cornelia herself had not been in the courtroom. Both court appearances took place a good while before Vatble was himself a citizen of the United States. He took his oath and paid the $2 fee in October 1844 and, having sworn his fidelity, offered it during the same court session in support of a fellow Frenchman, Achilles DuBourg.[16]

Her freedom confirmed, Cornelia could have children who would also be free. She and Conway had daughter Catherine in 1845. Son Lucien was born a year later, and another son, Richard, joined the family in 1849.[17]

Through Vatble, William Ratel gave Cornelia and all her progeny the gift of freedom, a gift she was smart enough to seek. Surrounded by slaves in both Lexington and Louisville, Cornelia understood that, whatever her personal experience, she was in dangerous territory. Her freedom papers provided significant, although incomplete, protection from a generally hostile white community. Conway and Cornelia, now differentiated from the city's slaves by their freedom and from other free people by their backgrounds, were advantaged among Louisville's African Americans, a fact that demanded prudence when dealing with their white neighbors. Free blacks, especially the successful, could be targets.

Like Cornelia, Conway understood his vulnerabilities in the world and took measures to protect himself. Both before and after his marriage, Conway worked on steamboats plying the river systems in the heart of the country. Sometime between 1845 and 1848, Robert Bell, an Irish steamboat clerk and pilot based in Louisville, purchased an insurance policy on Barbour from the Nautilus Insurance Company, the corporate ancestor of New York Life. Bell was an associate of Captain Monroe Quarrier, famous for rescuing passengers of the steamer *Tuscaloosa* after it caught fire in Mobile Bay in January 1847. In the late 1840s, co-owners Bell and Quarrier insured five slaves with Nautilus, and Quarrier insured six more he owned alone. Barbour was the only man insured by Bell as the sole owner and the only insured man with a surname on the policy. Barbour was identified in the paperwork as a "slave cabin boy," even though he was free and included in Louisville city directories as a resident of 291 Walnut Street, a property the Barbours rented for a few years and then purchased in 1850.[18]

Both Bell and Barbour would have had good reason to participate in this deception. Free blacks working on the rivers were easy prey for kidnappers, who could sell them as slaves. They were also unwelcome and subject to confinement while in port in some cities, including New Orleans. To evade the law, free blacks would sometimes ask an officer to pretend to be their owner. A wealthy free black businessman from Louisville complained that he could not send his children to Louisiana to shop unless he could find a white person to go with them and claim them as slaves. Pretending to be a slave allowed Barbour to avoid the indignity of jail time in New Orleans and saved his employers the bother of delivering him to and retrieving him from local authorities. And, according to the arrangement between Bell and Barbour, some or all of the insurance policy's proceeds might benefit Cornelia if Conway were killed on the river. This smart, if dishonest, deal between Barbour and Robert Bell indicates that they may have been friends; Conway accumulated many white allies during his life. The Nautilus policy and Cornelia's timely manumission suggest the Barbours understood that successful people of color in antebellum Louisville had to be flexible and creative in equal measure.[19]

———

Louisville's Market Revolution included major economic and civic projects in the second quarter of the nineteenth century that gave African Americans like Conway Barbour a shot at prosperity. The city's biggest problem was its foremost asset, the river itself. The Ohio River dropped precipitously at Louisville. The trip downstream was manageable in high water but troublesome in low; the trip upstream was treacherous or impossible all the time. The Louisville and Portland Canal, completed in 1830, fixed the problem for a while and sparked a growing steamboat culture that, for example, sent tobacco, hemp, and other goods south to New Orleans and brought sugar, coffee, and luxury items back from Europe. By the late 1840s, the canal was obsolete, owing to the increased size of steamboats, and the Falls of the Ohio River was again an issue. In the meanwhile, however, the canal brought increased trade and migration to or through Louisville. Two new hotels, the Louisville and the Galt, met the needs of transients. The former was regarded as the best in the city; the latter featured "pickaninnies" who cooled guests with peacock-feather fans. By midcentury, the population of the country's fourteenth-largest city exceeded 43,000, including 5,400 slaves and 1,500 free blacks.[20]

Growth had its costs as well as its benefits. Gamblers, thieves, and other ne'er-do-wells haunted the city's dark streets, preying primarily on migrants and their banknotes. Gaslights installed on some streets in the late 1830s were supposed to help curb crime but were better known for killing all the trees on Fourth Street with their noxious fumes. Railroad accidents and steamboat explosions also reminded folks of technology's risks. Disgusted with overzealous inventors everywhere, an anonymous Louisville satirist published plans for something called the Great Steam Duck, an airship shaped like a mallard that would allow a pilot to reconnoiter the river from above. Despite the skeptics, community infighting, and economic contractions, Louisville residents built a new city hall, banks, iron foundries, and other projects, ventures made possible in part with wealth produced by the steamboats. In 1850, civic booster Ben Casseday reported that fifty-three steamboats owned by Louisvillians employed more than 1,900 hands. Capital investment in the boats was worth $1.3 million; annual product for freight and passage, more than $2.5 million.[21]

Traditionally restricted to menial and service occupations, Louisville's African Americans gained access to new opportunities in the 1840s and 1850s. William Gibson, a free black musician and educator who moved from Baltimore to Louisville in the late 1840s, wrote a memoir decades later that described free black society in the antebellum period. He remembered Washington Spradling, of course, the very wealthy black barber, real estate mogul, and go-to guy for those in trouble. Gibson also mentioned by name other free black barbers, painters, carpenters, butchers, bricklayers, and tailors, among other professionals—men pushing their way into the middle class. Some of the best jobs were on the river, and free black men could earn relatively high wages and gain prestige among their peers by working as stewards, assistant stewards, or cooks on the increasingly pala-tial steamboats traveling the Ohio and Mississippi River systems. Gibson identified a dozen black stewards of the steamboat era, including Conway Barbour, as being prominent men in the African American community and respected by the citizenry in general.[22]

Because of their jobs on the steamboats, this small group of stewards rose toward the top of the black social hierarchy in Louisville. Gibson said Barbour, William and John Rankin, Dabney Page, and a few others acquired property and lived comfortably in their homes. They were also, however, "required to use discretion in their intercourse with their slave brethren." "Close conversation or undue familiarity" could cause suspicion. And if the slave escaped to Canada, Gibson wrote, "the freeman would probably be arrested as being connected with the Underground Railroad." Some years before the federal Fugitive Slave Act of 1850 alarmed free people of color throughout the country, these rivermen in Louisville negotiated an exhilarating and dangerous place on the edge of the slave system.[23]

The total number of hands employed on the Mississippi-Ohio River sys-tem at midcentury has been estimated at somewhere between fifteen and twenty thousand persons. If the workers on the ninety-three steamboats resting at St. Louis in 1850 were representative, approximately 6 percent, or up to 1,200 men and women, were free blacks, and about one-third of those were cabin crew. While any position in the cabin was desirable and cooks were respected among the small black middle class, the steward's position was the most prestigious. Dressed in suits or white coats, they wielded power on and off the boats.[24]

Since they supervised waiters and other members of the crew, stewards sometimes seemed impudent to white passengers and snobbish to other African Americans. Mark Twain wrote that "Negro" men working on high-end steamers were well aware of their relatively elevated status and often were eager to flaunt it. Conway Barbour, advertising his restaurant in Alton, Illinois, in the 1860s, bragged that he had more than thirty years' experience as a steward on the rivers' finest boats, a claim that reveals the pride he took in his service as a steward and the degree to which his identity was tied to his position and power on the boats.[25]

Tasked with stocking the larder before sailing and restocking along the way, stewards like Conway had to know where and from whom additional food and sundries might be procured. They often acquired these supplies from slaves and free blacks along the route, thereby serving as a conduit for information among enslaved and free people. If, as abolitionist and former slave William Wells Brown said, the crew's conversations were restricted aboard, those restraints fell away once ashore. Rivermen carried letters between family members, shared information on escape routes, and aided stowaways. More daring, some stewards and cooks hired fugitives to work on their staffs. Boatmen knew transit schedules and the names of those white officers unlikely to peruse the passes required of blacks. This made the watermen valuable assets to those seeking escape. The river and the rivermen posed a threat to the slave system.[26]

Steamboat owners were sometimes sued for "losing" slaves on the river or transporting runaways, and, as Gibson noted, free black steamboat workers were thought to be complicit in the escapes. Newspaper advertisements from the time demonstrate slave owners' fears that steamboat crews helped their property abscond, and the notices sometimes referred to specific boats when advertising runaways from Louisville and other cities along the Ohio and Mississippi Rivers. Free people of color generally, and especially rivermen, were more closely scrutinized after 1850 as racial tensions and the number of fugitives increased. Louisville's whites worried that the urban atmosphere and free black community assisted slaves headed north, and their fears were well founded. As Pamela R. Peters has shown, African Americans in slave-state Kentucky and free-state Indiana often interacted across the Ohio River. Louisville masters sent their slaves to New Albany to conduct business on their behalf; slaves and indentured servants from Floyd County, Indiana, were hired out in Louisville. Friendships, church ties, and fraternal bonds among blacks in both communities, many of them employed on steamboats, facilitated activity for the Underground Railroad. Not all free blacks were friends of the runaways; on occasion, they betrayed their enslaved brothers and sisters to local authorities. More often, however, free rivermen like Barbour quietly promoted the cause of freedom.[27]

The crewmen's primary motivation was more practical: work on the rivers paid well. At midcentury, stewards earned $50 a month or more at a time when pork, the staple meat, cost from three to five cents per pound and a dozen eggs sold for less than eight cents. Wages were highest on the large luxury boats running the distance trades between New Orleans and St. Louis or Louisville, like the steamer *Eclipse.* In the late 1840s and early 1850s, Barbour worked under Captain Zack Shirley on the steamboat *Fashion,* which ran between Louisville and St. Louis. Wife Cornelia was left in Louisville much of the time with their children and a house to tend on Walnut Street. Hers was not always an easy job.[28]

Despite the Barbours' status in the African American community, Cornelia had to contend with the challenges of being both a free person of color in a slave society and a woman whose husband was often absent. When disrespected, however, she fought back. Her sense of self—a product of her early years in a refined atmosphere, easy emancipation, and marriage to a prominent steward—equipped her with the tools to defend herself when necessary.

S. G. Henry's Auction and Commission Rooms at the corner of Main and Wall Streets advertised itself as the place for "good goods and good bargains." With regular auctions every Tuesday and Friday, the auctioneer and commission merchant sold its wares to the highest bidder for cash or in private sales. On 11 October 1849, Cornelia Barbour sued Samuel G. Henry and William P. Shepherd in Jefferson County court for defrauding her of household goods that included a cooking stove worth $12; a card table, $6; another table, $6; twenty-five yards of carpet, $8; curtains, $4; stone jars, $4; and a large map, $10. According to the suit, she had "lost" goods that came into the possession of the defendants, who knew they belonged to her but would not return them.[29]

In an era when abolitionist tracts and newspapers were confiscated and free blacks were presumed to be aiding fugitive slaves, perhaps her purchase of the map raised eyebrows. She was, after all, married to a riverman. Henry and Shepherd may have presumed the map would be used for illegal purposes, or they may have taken all the furnishings simply because they believed they could. In what may have been a metaphoric battle over the caste system or a case of simple fraud, Cornelia was a woman deprived of those things that make a house her own. She sued for $50 in damages. Among those summoned to testify on her behalf was Aristide Vatble, the man who had freed her several years earlier.

The court documents refer to the merchants' offense as trespass. Possibly the goods were stolen from her and turned up as good bargains in a regularly scheduled auction, or perhaps she paid for goods that Henry and Shepherd would not deliver. In any event, the items were never returned to her. The case was continued four times in 1850 and finally dismissed in March 1851. Cornelia lost her case, but the fact that she pursued it in court suggests she had no fear of standing up for herself against the vastly stronger forces of white mercantilism. That she fought alone in this struggle—Conway is not mentioned in any of the court documents—demonstrates the power she had within her own family and her independent spirit.

That she fought at all shows that the Barbours felt themselves entitled, as productive free citizens, to equal protection under the law.

In Kentucky, however, free people of color were by statute inferior to whites and generally without the protection the Barbours expected. The state's 1792 constitution gave free blacks the vote, but a new version in 1799 revoked the privilege. Free blacks were subject to many provisions of the slave code such that capital crimes for slaves were also capital crimes for freemen. Lesser crimes meant fines, imprisonment, or the whip. Hiding a slave merited a punishment of up to twenty lashes; writing a pass or free papers for a slave could put a free man in prison for years. The courts allowed free blacks to pursue misdemeanor cases, like Cornelia's suit against S. G. Henry, but they could not testify against whites in any legal proceeding. Free black Kentuckians had the right to jury trial and could provide evidence on their own behalf, but they could only sometimes object in jury selection and only sometimes use the right of appeal. The state did not explicitly forbid the education of blacks, but most who received training did so in private or church schools, despite the state school taxes required of their parents.[30]

Local ordinances were harsh, arbitrary, and made precarious the line between free and enslaved. Free men and women singled out as loiterers or purveyors of alcohol could be fined or jailed. Those unable to produce on command proof of their freedom risked being jailed and advertised as runaways. Free blacks were also subject to local patrols that could burst into their homes, ostensibly in search of fugitives or stolen goods, ransack at will, and take whatever they wanted without consequence. In perhaps the worst humiliation, free men without gainful employment could be hired out—enslaved, that is—by local law enforcement.[31]

Codified oppression, however, was not enough to frustrate the ambitions of some free blacks, like the Barbours, who built families, careers, and communities despite the restrictions, sometimes with the help of white friends. The Fourth Street Colored Methodist Church (Asbury Chapel), which invited Gibson to Louisville in 1847, held Sunday school classes under white supervision and had on file hundreds of permission slips from masters allowing their slaves to be educated. Officers of several black churches organized a children's choir that performed on Sunday afternoons, and Gibson participated in a racially mixed orchestra. He also recalled, however, that accomplished black guitarist Samuel L. White was harassed by whites for being too refined. When White appealed to local authorities for help, he was advised to leave the state.[32]

Lacking support from Louisville officialdom, the black community took care of its own. Spradling complained that, except in cases of smallpox, no official resources were available for sick blacks. Friends raised the money needed to bury African Americans who died without property. Much of the work was done through black churches that sponsored common schools, collected libraries, and policed the behavior of congregants in open forums where all members, slave and free, had a vote.[33]

Conway Barbour, unlike many African Americans of his era and since, apparently had little interest in organized religion. Although his family can be found on church membership lists, his name never appears. "C. Barber," listed as part of the Methodist John Wesley Temple (Center Street Church) in the 1848 Louisville city directory, was probably Clark Barbour, the former slave of Richard Barbour, a member of the large, white Barbour family. Clark and Conway were connected through the white Barbours but probably not related. Years later, Clark's son Richard, fresh from service in the Civil War, stayed in Conway's hotel, indicating an ongoing relationship between the two families. A shared appreciation of religion was unlikely a part of the tie.[34]

Rivermen like Barbour tended to be a secular group. Life on the water was a manly venture, involving a lot of drinking, gambling, and brawling. In 1845, for example, steward Lewis Springer sued Captain Quarrier for choking him until he was blue and "looked like a corpse." Quarrier broke up a fight between Springer and an unnamed chambermaid by squeezing the steward's neck until the skin came off. An unsympathetic court awarded the aggrieved steward one penny. In that work environment, attempts by Christian groups to save the souls of boatmen were often rebuffed, and Barbour was apparently among the skeptics. Evidence suggests that, while Barbour sought elevation in the world, he did not pursue it through the church, an important gateway for many other ambitious African Americans. Barbour served as witness to a wedding in Louisville's Catholic Cathedral of the Assumption, Vatble's church, on 17 August 1850, but that appears to be the extent of his churchgoing.[35]

With or without church ties, Conway and Cornelia Barbour were established, prominent members of Louisville's black community in the late 1840s. Even so, the Barbours were not immune to the abuse inflicted by whites on their unwelcome class. Kentucky's racial history compared favorably with points farther south, but for the state's free blacks and slaves, the difference served only to demonstrate their peril. Things could always get worse. And they did.

The increasingly heated national debate over slavery in the late 1840s put the fates of all people of color in flux, as attacks on and defenses of the institution necessarily begged the question of the role of free blacks in America. In the South, relatively successful free blacks like the Barbours could overhear, but not participate in, this discussion of their future. The consequences for them were both existential and unclear when white Kentucky decided to rewrite its state constitution.

Although more than 70 percent of white households in Kentucky owned no slaves in 1850, and slaveholding was so geographically concentrated that many white Kentuckians barely had contact with the institution, the majority supported it and had done so since the commonwealth was carved out of slaveholding Virginia. Presbyterians tried and failed to excise slavery from the state constitution in 1792; Baptists tried and failed in 1799.[36]

Unable to envision whites living among large numbers of black freedmen, antislavery Kentuckians like Henry Clay formed the Kentucky Colonization Society in 1829, although its efforts were largely a failure. Only 661 black Kentuckians immigrated to Africa in the entire antebellum period. Primarily worried about slavery's impact on economic development—namely, white labor—antislavery conservatives focused on colonization and thus avoided what would have been a futile, direct challenge to slavery itself. In this way they could appeal to those who favored emancipation, to those who were proslavery, and to those who simply wanted blacks removed from the state.[37]

Meanwhile, antislavery rhetoric also found its voice in Kentuckians Cassius M. Clay and John G. Fee. Abolitionist, missionary, and pacifist, Fee was dragged from his pulpit so often that his daughter grew up thinking mobs were as common as thunderstorms: "We supposed everybody had mobs." Yale-educated Clay, himself a wealthy slave owner, began his antislavery career advocating the conservatives' economic argument. He published a newspaper, *True American*, before leaving for the Mexican-American War. Thereafter, Louisville's antislavery leadership took over the publication, renaming it the *Examiner*. That newspaper and others followed closely a court case in Louisville in 1848 that reflected rising tension in the country following the war.[38]

The Mexican-American War was critical to the slavery debate in the United States and the coming of the Civil War. With the Treaty of Guadalupe-Hidalgo in February 1848, the United States grew a third again in size to the west at Mexico's expense, and the natural question for southerners rallied to support the war by the Wilmot Proviso was whether they could take their "property" into the newly acquired territories. From 1848 until the Civil War, the problem before the country was the expansion of slavery into these territories. For southerners, it became a question of citizenship. Southern blood lay on the ground in Texas as did northern blood. Massachusetts men could take their property to New Mexico. If South Carolina men could not take theirs, they would become second-class citizens, an unacceptable assault on their manhood and on American citizenship, or so they thought. Their defense of their way of life became more strident, and control of both slaves and free blacks seemed crucial.

In October 1848, Peter Roberts, a free man of color, was auctioned at the Jefferson County, Kentucky, courthouse for $75.50. Roberts had been charged with violating a law that forbade free blacks from remaining in the state for more than thirty days. Roberts, a Methodist preacher and a Mason, claimed to reside across the Ohio River in Jeffersonville, Indiana, with his wife and children. Earlier in the year, he rented a barbershop in Louisville. He worked in his shop during the day and returned to Indiana at night. Roberts's attorneys argued that the state law violated the privileges and immunities clause of the U.S. Constitution, which holds that citizens of each state are entitled to the rights they have in any other state. In the Roberts case, Judge William Bullock declared that free blacks were not citizens of any state and unprotected by the Constitution. Therefore, Roberts was auctioned and purchased by Isaac L. Hyatt, a coal merchant. The state law was later declared unconstitutional and Roberts released, but in the meanwhile the case focused national attention on the rights of free blacks. The *North Star* said, "it would be well" if a similar case went before the U.S. Supreme Court so that the meaning of the privileges and immunities clause "might be expounded." When that happened in 1857, Chief Justice Roger Taney declared that African Americans were not and could not be U.S. citizens.[39]

Around the time Roberts was freed, Kentucky's proslavery forces engineered a repeal of the state law prohibiting the importation of slaves from other states, and both sides of the issue began calling for a constitutional convention. Ostensibly the proposed constitutional revision would fix undemocratic elements of the 1799 version, but once the electorate approved the multiyear process, slavery became the main issue. Newspapers, such as the new *Louisville Chronicle*, were created solely for the purpose of opposing emancipation, while others, including the *Courier*, went on record as favoring the move. Louisville's mechanics and workingmen adopted a resolution calling for slavery's "ultimate extinction" since the institution was one that "degrades labor."[40]

On 11 October 1849, the *National Era* reprinted a hopeful article from the *Louisville Examiner* touting the strength of emancipationist sentiment in the city. While pro-emancipation delegates to the constitutional convention received only about 10 percent of the total vote, they garnered 45 percent in Louisville. Their political preference carried a cost, however. During elections in the city, some antislavery voters were physically assaulted, and a gun battle between proslavery voters and antislavery election observers resulted in two casualties.[41]

Violence and the 1849 cholera outbreak complicated the election process, but in the end, antislavery voices, always divided over how to achieve their goals, weakened while proslavery forces coalesced. The new state constitution proclaimed the right to own slaves as "before and higher than any constitutional sanction" and required that payment be made to anyone capturing a fugitive. It also sought to limit the number of free blacks by making manumission more difficult and by requiring those freed after the passage of the new constitution to leave the state. Slavery was to be permanent in Kentucky.[42]

The new constitution made clear that people of African American descent were unwelcome in Kentucky and that free blacks like the Barbours would be forever at risk. Neither Conway's property, nor his job, nor his last name would necessarily protect him and his family from a white person who decided to cause trouble. Never friendly to free blacks, Louisville now sought to restrict or eliminate their presence altogether.

As if to emphasize the point, the new state constitution prompted Louisville authorities to revise the city's slave code and put new restrictions on all people of color. After 1851, all buildings used by blacks of the city had to be approved and licensed by the city council. The hours that black churches could be open were limited, and events scheduled for days other than Sunday or Wednesday required official sanction. The hardened slave code and hardening proslavery attitudes meant that behavior once considered beneath the conduct of gentlemen became more commonplace. According to one account, "We saw more frequently negro gangs driven through the city. Formerly, a man [slave driver] didn't like to be seen in that position, but . . . it became common to drive gangs of slaves through the streets, and they made public exhibitions of it." Such demonstrations of racial power and flagrant cruelty would certainly have affected free blacks differentiated from those in the coffles by mere pieces of paper.[43]

Their anxiety grew. Gibson said many free blacks responded to the deteriorating conditions by leaving town, especially after a proposal was floated to bind out free black children to white employers. Although the measure failed, its implications frightened free families, and, according to Gibson, "an exodus took place." Census data contradict his assertion. The number of free blacks in Louisville increased by almost four hundred between 1850 and 1860, even as the number of manumissions declined.[44]

Although Conway and Cornelia Barbour might have shared the general uneasiness of their friends and neighbors, because of their ties to community, they were not compelled to flee in panic. The steamboat steward was privileged to gather intelligence and chart his future with deliberation. Perhaps he surveyed Ohio's possibilities during an anniversary celebration of West Indies Emancipation Day in Cincinnati or Cleveland. Maybe Gibson told him about hearing Frederick Douglass speak at the Free-Soil Convention in Pittsburgh in 1852. On the river, Barbour would have had access to abolitionist tracts and antislavery newspapers, although it was a dangerous business. Gibson had his copies of *Frederick Douglass' Paper* mailed to a friend in Indiana and hid the issues in the top of a piano once he had read them. Barbour might have read the papers or the published adventures of former slaves Henry Bibb and William Wells Brown. Few were unaware of *Uncle Tom's Cabin.* The politics of slavery produced an avalanche of words in the two decades before the Civil War, including accounts of the conventions of "colored" people held almost annually after 1849.[45]

Conway Barbour wanted to be a part of the national conversation on the future of America's blacks. Embracing his racial distinction, Barbour became interested in Martin Delany's emigration movement. He was Kentucky's representative to the National Emigration Convention of Colored People in Cleveland in August 1854, and he moved his family to the city a little more than a year later. Political ambition, however, was not his only reason for relocating Cornelia and the children. He was trying to conceal his double life.

TWO

Cleveland

IN AN ERA that strictly limited the political participation of black men, the convention movement provided an opportunity for leadership in a space energized by righteous grievance and hope. Historian Patrick Rael saw the conventions as part of a protest movement that both taught and evoked northern culture and values to challenge the caste system from within. Like R. J. Young, Rael found important racial and demographic differences between blacks who attended the conventions and those they wanted to lead. Indeed, Young argues that the most important difference was not between "assimilationists and separatists" but between the activists and other African Americans. Were it not for the rigidity of race, in this view, black elites who identified with white middle-class values might have left their poorer friends behind. Pervasive hostility was the centripetal force.[1]

For Conway Barbour, Martin Delany's National Emigration Convention of Colored People was an opportunity to weigh in on the existential questions before his race and to make a name for himself among some better-known men. In Cleveland, he could test an idea that his future was not on the rivers but in convention halls or even statelier buildings, the kind in which his white Barbour relatives did business. Playing with possibility, Barbour took a leap even as the country veered toward disaster.

In 1854, Illinois senator Stephen Douglas, invested in dreams of both the presidency and Chicago real estate, sought to enrich the country and possibly himself with a transcontinental railroad along a northerly route. The concept of a transcontinental rail had been around since the end of the Mexican-American War in 1848, but the issue was tied up in controversy over the expansion of slavery into the newly acquired territories. California's bid for statehood after the 1849 gold rush produced crisis and the unsatisfying Compromise of 1850, which kept the peace for a while but left fundamental issues unresolved. To facilitate the railroad, Douglas introduced the Kansas-Nebraska Act with the question of slavery left up to the "popular sovereignty" of the territories' residents.

Proslavery southerners seized on the contradiction between popular sovereignty, which might decide in favor of slavery, and the hard geographic line set by the Missouri Compromise of 1820. In exchange for their support of the legislation, the southerners demanded specific repeal of the "sacred" Missouri Compromise line, and Douglas agreed, arguing that the concession meant little. Kansas and Nebraska folk would reject slavery, Douglas assured his northern friends, because the institution would not pay in that climate. The bill passed, and, predictably, both sides of the slavery issue sent armies to Kansas for a civil war several years before the Civil War. The violence was just getting under way as Barbour listened to Delany make the case that America's blacks should simply remove themselves from the tumult.

The Cleveland convention was the pinnacle of the antebellum emigration movement, or what has been called "the search for a black nationality." Recognizing that people of African descent were not then and probably never would be accepted by white society, some free blacks called for a new beginning outside the United States. Differing fundamentally from the white founders of the American Colonization Society and its state adjuncts, black emigrationists rejected the racism associated with whites' removal plans, while retaining and elaborating the notion that they would be better off with people of similar cultural and racial heritage. The movement waxed and waned in the Early Republic as settlement efforts fell apart before reaching fruition or failed outright. In the 1830s, even as blacks and whites worked together in the growing abolitionist movement, Pennsylvania minister Lewis Woodson joined the concepts of emigration and nationalism and urged blacks to leave the country as a demonstration of independent power. In the 1850s, Delany, Woodson's student, advocated creating a nation of former Americans who would work closely with other black people around the globe. Delany ultimately retreated from this position, but the emigrationist response to American racism reappeared later, most notably in the movement led by Marcus Garvey.[2]

Born in Charlestown, Virginia, in 1812, Delany was a barber and physician who became involved in moral reform, particularly temperance, in Pittsburgh, Pennsylvania. A political activist in the 1840s, he edited the *Mystery* from 1843 to 1847, the only black newspaper published in Pennsylvania at the time. He partnered with Frederick Douglass on the *North Star* for two years after giving up the *Mystery*, lecturing and seeking subscriptions to the paper before resigning in 1849. A critic of the American Colonization Society, Delany also condemned those blacks he thought to be impoverished because of their own moral deficiencies. Central to his argument was the idea that blacks could elevate themselves in society by seeking higher occupations and rejecting religious tenets that fostered servility. When it became apparent to him that American society abused all blacks regardless of their industriousness and respectability, Delany moved toward emigration and black nationalism.[3]

In 1852, he published *The Condition, Elevation, Emigration and Destiny of the Colored People of the United States, Politically Considered*, a tract that urged blacks to seek other areas of the Americas for resettlement. The piece also denounced white abolitionists as hypocrites who failed to give blacks the jobs they needed to prosper. Blacks, Delany argued, should lead themselves out of the desert and into a promised land south of the Rio Grande, possibly after a detour through Canada. Although other black leaders agreed with those elements of Delany's *Condition* that implied black pride, they would not follow him beyond the national border. Delany's call for a national emigration convention in Cleveland in August 1854 was, therefore, a pivotal moment in the antebellum debate among African Americans on the proper solution to America's racial issues.[4]

Abandoning home and hearth had little appeal to most African Americans, despite their oppression. Many, including Douglass, found the call for emigration to be little more than a betrayal. Advocacy of emigration suggested that blacks, as many whites said, had no right to be in the United States. *Frederick Douglass' Paper* printed Delany's announcement of the convention but thereafter would not support it, and instead the paper published letters calling Delany's project misguided. Even so, for Delany and other black emigrationists, the question was not *whether* African Americans should leave but rather *where* they should go. Delany preferred the West Indies or Central or South America.[5]

In the first half of the nineteenth century, Americans held local, state, or national meetings on almost any topic of the day, and African Americans enthusiastically participated in this cultural phenomenon. In the three decades before the Civil War, blacks held eleven national conventions, more than thirty state conventions, and an untold number of local meetings. These were northerners meeting in northern venues to complain about their treatment in northern "free" states.[6]

When westerners became more prominent in the movement in the late 1840s, the agenda and goals advanced at the conventions became more militant. By the early 1850s, earlier demands for self-expression and moral uplift had evolved into a more radical approach that sometimes strained the relationship between black and white abolitionists. After the Compromise of 1850, calls for violent racial defense within the United States or removal from the country—emigration—intensified. Many African American writers and editors who had previously rejected emigration now embraced it, although they disagreed among themselves about the details. Some black spokesmen advocated emigration for individual self-advancement but did not endorse an organized exodus. Some of this view took their own advice. So many prominent African Americans lived outside the United States in the early 1850s that emigration appeared to be more popular than it was for average blacks. Even so, Elizabeth Rauh Bethel asserts that an estimated 20 percent of the free black population left the United States between 1820 and 1860.[7]

The trend was disturbing for men like Douglass, who maintained that free blacks should fight for themselves and their enslaved countrymen at home. Sensing the momentum building for emigration, Douglass and his followers announced an elaborate plan for race-based self-help organizations at an 1853 national convention in Rochester, New York, and openly condemned Delany's announcement of the emigration convention the following year. The Ohio meeting generated so much controversy that a separate publication was distributed exploring the plan to convene: *Arguments, Pro and Con, on the Call for a National Convention to Be Held in Cleveland, Ohio, August 24, 1854.*[8]

When Conway Barbour traveled north to the Congregational church on Prospect Street that summer, he became a part of this debate.

In order to participate, aspiring delegates needed only to show up and affirm support for the cause to the credentials committee. Of the 101 delegates to the convention, only six, including Barbour, represented slave states. H. Ford Douglas and Lawrence Minor represented Louisiana (New Orleans), although both men were Ohio residents as late as 1850; Douglas in Cleveland, Minor in Cincinnati. Charles Starks and Edward Butler hailed from St. Louis; Peter Lowery represented Tennessee. Barbour was the lone delegate from Kentucky. About half of the delegates were from Delany's Pittsburgh or nearby. A handful of the participants were well known, but for many it was their first and last participation in racial politics.[9]

The *Proceedings*, published later in 1854, characterized many of the speeches given during the convention's three days. Delany delivered a short but touching eulogy on recently deceased Henry Bibb, author of a famous escape narrative. H. Ford Douglas's comment on Delany's "State Paper" titled "Political Destiny of the Colored Race on the American Continent" was described as "able and eloquent," demonstrating "a gigantic mind, commanding oratory, and an . . . intellect of no ordinary degree." John Mercer Langston's lengthy speech was "replete with classic elegance" and was answered by Douglas with a "withering sarcasm" that "kept the house in a ferment of emotion." Reverend Augustus Green's remarks were "judicious." After suspension of the rules, both Barbour and Lowery of Tennessee were allowed to speak, but the content of their remarks was neither recorded nor described in the *Proceedings*, and the two southerners appeared only in lists elsewhere in the convention record. Barbour was on the business committee that ostensibly aided in the preparation of Delany's state paper, but the document was really Delany's work alone.[10]

Even so, Barbour was named Louisville's representative on a newly formed national board of commissioners, an honor that suggested the potential benefits to be derived from association with the movement. Taking his new position seriously, Barbour nominated his friend William Gibson to serve on the same board and tried to have his own name corrected in the transactions of the meeting. The misspelling of Barbour's name in the early pages of the *Proceedings*, "Conaway Barber," was noted in an erratum at the end of the document.[11]

Opposition to the emigration movement persisted, and even Delany began to modify his views. By the time the national commissioners met in Pittsburgh in August 1855, Delany had softened toward the idea of Canadian settlements and earned the support of previously skeptical Mary Ann Shadd, publisher of the *Provincial Freeman* at Chatham. Delany moved to Chatham in early 1856, some months before the second emigration convention was to convene in Cleveland. That second meeting was much smaller than the first one; even Delany was absent due to illness. A new national board roster, published in the 25 November 1856 *Provincial Freeman*, was greatly reduced compared with two years earlier. In addition to four officers and six national-level members, the board consisted of nine representatives from just five states: Connecticut, New York, Ohio, Michigan, and New Jersey. Barbour's name appeared neither in the abstract and summary of the meeting nor on the national board list.[12]

Barbour's brief foray into emigration politics was over. He had always been more interested in politics than emigration in any case, and he was not at all interested in leaving the country. Participation in the convention fed his ego and gave him ideas. He liked what he saw in Cleveland. A tornado hit Louisville just as he returned home; tensions between immigrant laborers and Know-Nothings were worsening and would boil over on "Bloody Monday" a year later. And then there was the daily worry that went with being a free black man in a slave society.[13]

In October 1856, Conway contracted with Cleveland real estate agent James Kilbreth for two town lots and purchased three more parcels from developer Joseph Lyman the following July. Barbour already owned rural acreage to the northeast, in Lake County, Ohio, but chose to relocate to the urban area. The homestead on Case Avenue in the eastern part of the city included a frame house and barn valued at $1,500 in 1860. Meanwhile, Conway brought Cornelia, again pregnant, and the children north. A son, Edward, was born in Cleveland in 1857.[14]

The city had a reputation among free blacks as being more welcoming than most areas of Ohio, and it was an important stop for blacks, free and enslaved, seeking to cross into Canada. While it was not the oasis for people of color that some historians have suggested, it might have seemed so to the Barbours.

Ohio's racial history was shaped by its geographic location. Although article 6 of the Northwest Ordinance of 1787 prohibited slavery north of the Ohio River, the law was interpreted such that slaves could be found in Illinois and Indiana into the mid-nineteenth century. For those who favored slavery in the Old Northwest Territory, article 6 was said to be a prohibition on the importation of *new* slaves into the region; existing slaves were thought to be unaffected. This was the opinion of territorial governor Arthur St. Clair and a stance to which George Washington acquiesced. Proslavery and antislavery white residents agreed on their antipathy to blacks generally, and very early in Ohio state history, legislators enacted laws intended to exclude blacks, both slave and free, or at least to minimize their number.[15]

Under the ordinances, free blacks were allowed to vote and did so in the 1802 campaign for a state constitutional convention. The convention then wrote a document that denied African American suffrage. The antislavery plank passed by only one vote. Blacks and mulattos were not to be counted for the purpose of determining representation or appropriation of funds, but the new constitution did not specifically restrict militia duty, jury trial, or access to education by race. It did not directly provide for these rights either. This ambiguity gave racists an opportunity to clarify their position.

Southern Ohioans with economic ties to southern states feared that a liberal racial policy would hurt business. As a sign of goodwill, therefore, legislators excluded blacks from the militia in 1803. The following year, blacks were required to show proof on demand of their free status, to register with their county, and to pay a fee of twelve and a half cents per person when doing so. In 1807, a revised black code compelled blacks to arrange a bond with at least two property owners to ensure good behavior, and it denied them the right to testify in any court case in which either party was white.[16]

By the 1820s, the Ohio legislature restricted slave catching within state borders but also put up barriers to African American employment and education. An 1829 law for white-only education was modified in 1849 to allow segregated or, in some cases, mixed schools, but in the intervening two decades, blacks paid taxes for schools their children could not attend. As in most of the Old Northwest, the black codes of Ohio were selectively enforced, especially the registration laws. Only 401 African Americans were registered in Cuyahoga County between 1832 and 1837, and none thereafter. Later registries may have been lost or were not maintained in the first place. Periodic crackdowns, usually the result of an increasing black population and visibility, brought violence, most infamously in Cincinnati in 1829 and in Portsmouth in 1830.[17]

The atmosphere in Ohio underwent a metamorphosis after the 1830s as antislavery activism and political competition opened new opportunities for voices urging repeal of the state's black laws. Conservatives remained concerned that repeal would mean even more blacks in the state, but especially after the Mexican-American War, the code was linked to the extension of slavery. In 1849, a year after Cleveland hosted a national convention of "colored freemen," a coalition of Democrats and Free-Soilers pushed through repeal of the state's immigration and testimony laws as well as a revision of the racial rules for education.[18]

Although most Ohio politicians opposed the federal Fugitive Slave Act of 1850, the legislature voted down a proposal to criminalize its enforcement in the state. Instead, the act produced a "bitter struggle" between Ohio and Kentucky over fugitive-slave cases in the 1850s. The law was most unpopular in Ohio's northern counties. At a Cleveland meeting, opponents declared parts of the Fugitive Slave Act to be unconstitutional and "the whole of it oppressive, unjust, and unrighteous." Cleveland, however, was more liberal than most of Ohio on racial matters.[19]

African Americans in Cleveland were "almost equal" before 1870, according to one historian. Although racial prejudice was apparent in the Forest City, blacks benefited from access to public facilities and jobs and from the disinclination of white authorities to enforce the state's black laws, at least after the 1830s. Over time, northern Ohio became a leader in both abolition and the push for equal rights, two goals frequently disconnected or in contention elsewhere.[20]

The number of African Americans in Cleveland grew slowly until the midcentury. In 1850, blacks were 1.3 percent of the city's population and numbered only 224 out of a total population of 17,034. By 1860, there were 799 African Americans in Cleveland, 1.9 percent of the city's population and the highest percentage until 1920. They enjoyed many integrated public facilities and, by the late 1840s, schools. Only New Orleans offered more opportunity, and African Americans responded to Cleveland's reputation: most of Cleveland's African American heads of household in 1860 were born in the South.[21]

Few Ohio-born blacks were prominent among Cleveland's African Americans. Southerners owned most of the real estate wealth, with natives of Virginia and North Carolina among the most prosperous. Barber John Brown and steamboat steward Asha Parker, both born in Virginia, reported $5,000 and $6,000, respectively, in property in 1860. Cicero Richardson's real estate was worth $5,000. Richardson, born in North Carolina, was a plasterer supporting a household of ten people. Another southerner, Susan Reynolds, was the largest property owner in the county in 1860 and for two decades thereafter. The ten-year-old Reynolds, "a charming mulatto girl with a head of long black curls," was the daughter of a Mississippi cotton planter and a slave woman. Ms. Reynolds lived at the corner of Prospect and Erie Streets with five servants and property valued at $40,000 in 1860.[22]

Native Ohioans and northern-born blacks, with some exceptions, did not fare as well financially, and the relative standing of all African Americans in Cleveland deteriorated over time. The percentage of blacks in service, unskilled, and semiskilled jobs grew from 29.5 percent in 1850 to more than 53 percent by 1870. Denied employment in Cleveland's burgeoning industrial sector, African Americans saw their occupational opportunities and property ownership diminish between 1850 and 1880.[23]

Clearly, Cleveland was no "Negro Paradise." The city's best theatre would seat blacks only in the balcony; its streetcars were segregated until late in the Civil War; and "colored" barbers who wanted to serve white customers dare not serve black ones. The liberal Cleveland *Herald* was shocked by a dinner at Oberlin attended by men and women of both races; the *Plain Dealer* declared that such demonstrations of social equality would "amalgamate the races and make this a government of minks and monkeys." These insults and indignities paled in comparison to legal discrimination in city courts that punished crimes committed by blacks harshly and those committed against them leniently. Nonetheless, compared with other parts of Ohio and the nation, Cleveland offered opportunities for personal advancement, particularly for southern-born blacks like Barbour.[24]

If Cleveland's reputation for racial tolerance was exaggerated, the city was still a marked improvement over Louisville, where Barbour's neighbors were enslaved and free blacks were subjected to raids by the patrols and other abuses. Cleveland's African Americans did not have to hide their newspapers in a piano. The city's blacks openly aired their grievances and participated in the many conventions of "colored" citizens of Ohio convened between 1849 and 1858, in addition to Delany's 1854 emigration meeting. Cleveland's delegation to the latter included Madison Tilly, a wealthy businessman who was at various times a Whig, a Republican, and a Democrat; William Howard Day, a graduate of Oberlin and the publisher of Cleveland's first black paper, the *Aliened American* (1853–55); and John Malvin.[25]

––––––––

Malvin and Barbour had a great deal in common. Both men were born in Virginia, pursued politics and business, and relocated repeatedly in search of success. Although both men attended the emigration convention, Barbour's commitment to the cause was shallow, and Malvin apparently wanted to talk about other issues. According to the *Proceedings*, Malvin asked Delany on the first day of the meeting if he would allow any remarks that "did not tend to Emigration," and the answer was no. Although he was instrumental in establishing a separate school for blacks in Cleveland in the early 1830s, Malvin was an integrationist whose work on behalf of African Americans earned him the moniker "Father John."[26]

Born free in Virginia in 1795, Malvin removed to Cincinnati in the late 1820s, only to find his status little elevated by residence in free territory.

While in Cincinnati, he was active in the Underground Railroad and helped draw up a petition to the state legislature demanding repeal of Ohio's black laws, a petition that was repudiated by members of the city's black Methodist Episcopal Church. Claiming to represent two hundred of the Queen City's African Americans, church leaders certified that they had no part in the petition and asked only for "a continuation of the smiles of the white people as we have hitherto enjoyed them." Such deference did not stave off racial violence that same summer, when white mobs forced more than 1,200 blacks to flee Cincinnati for Canada.[27]

Shortly thereafter, Malvin and his new wife moved to the Louisville area, where he worked as a carpenter. At one point, he was arrested as a suspected fugitive but was released after being roughly handled. Around 1830, he left his wife in Kentucky and headed for Canada to contract for a farm. On their way back to Canada, his wife developed misgivings about leaving her enslaved father in Louisville. "It lay so heavily upon her that she gave me no rest," Malvin wrote, and so they settled in Cleveland.[28]

Malvin's experience in Cleveland demonstrates the inconsistency of race relations in the city at the time. He had been able to obtain work as a carpenter in Louisville, but his race precluded him from plying the same trade in Cleveland. He took a job on a schooner and then at a mill where white coworkers shut off water to the boilers in an attempt to frame him for the anticipated explosion. A city functionary denied Malvin a business license to operate a boat he had purchased, but the decision was overruled by a superior. A charter member of the city's racially mixed First Baptist Church, Malvin fought with the congregation for eighteen months before it agreed to open seating for African Americans. As Malvin told it, Cleveland's blacks could obtain their rights, but they had to fight for them. The difference between Louisville and Cleveland was that racial attitudes in the southern city were hardening as those in the Forest City were relaxing.[29]

When the Barbours bought their home on Case Avenue, they became one of only three African American families in the Seventh Ward. Barbour's next-door neighbor, Reuben Foot, thirty-eight, a blacksmith from Virginia, owned a home worth $1,100 in 1860. Beverly Foot, forty, a gardener born in Mississippi, rented a couple of doors down. The steward Conway Barbour reported $1,500 in real property, but no personal property, in the Cleveland census in 1860; he reported $1,000 in real and $200 in personal property in the Alton, Illinois, census of the same year. Barbour appeared in two censuses because he was claimed by two wives.

On 2 January 1859, Reverend J. P. Corrington married Conway Barbour and Frances Rankin in Alton, and an announcement appeared in the *Alton Weekly Courier* a few days later. The newspaper identified Barbour as being from Kentucky, although he had not lived there for about three years, and Miss Rankin as being "of this city," that is, Alton. By the time the census was taken in 1860, their household included one-year-old Frances, called "Fannie"; Matilda Rankin, Frances's mother; and a twelve-year-old boy, Thomas, born in Kentucky in 1848 when Frances was fifteen and Conway was about twice that age. Conway Barbour, who had been having an affair with the younger sister of his fellow stewards from Louisville, was now a bigamist.[30]

Although it was illegal in all states, bigamy was not uncommon in the antebellum years. Most closely associated with Mormonism and other utopian sects, the practice was also part of broader, mainstream American society. Reported incidents were so common, wrote the editors of the *Chicago Tribune* in 1857, that "an outside barbarian would suppose . . . that at least one tenet of the Mormon faith was greatly in vogue in this country." Some stories were fairly straightforward. Authorities from Troy, New York, working on behalf of "Wife No. 1," tracked down Nelson B. Ells in Port Byron, Illinois, where he was living with "Wife No. 2." Others were more colorful. James Bennett, arrested in Jerseyville, Illinois, in 1854, ran off from Lexington, Kentucky, after squandering his wife's property, about $8,000. Passing himself off as both wealthy and single, he married a "widow lady" in Jerseyville but was discovered after "some persons" inquired to Lexington about his character. Since leaving Kentucky, the press reported, he had married at least two other women, one each in Iowa and Indiana. The Abney men, father and son, were both sentenced to Vermont state prison for bigamy in 1857. The "boy" had two wives; his father had six. Nathaniel J. Bird, alias Dr. William Hunter, held in jail at Camden, New Jersey, was visited by two of his wives on the same day. In short order, three more women came forward. When pressed, the twenty-three-year-old man claimed to have twenty wives, a statement, one newspaper said, "which may be true as more than one fourth of that number has been found in a few days." Bigamist Dayton Daniels, confronted with the case against him, tried several different defenses. He said that he was a minor at the time of his first marriage, that he was drunk, that he heard his first wife was dead, that there was no legal evidence of either of his marriages, and finally, that he meant no harm and so should be acquitted. He got three months in prison. One female bigamist, a Mrs. Erdman of Philadelphia, lived with Mr. Erdman for four years before running off and marrying a Mr. Bowman. Tiring of him after a few weeks, she "deserted him for the man with whom she was found when arrested."[31]

Some African Americans' marital histories were complicated by slavery. For example, civil rights activist Reverend Byrd Parker, accused of bigamy in 1854, argued that his first marriage was not binding because he was a slave at the time and could not legally make the contract. The cases of free blacks differed little from those of their white neighbors. A black preacher named Green, tried and convicted for bigamy in New York in 1847, had "three sable wives." Richard Barbour, Clark Barbour's son, married but did not divorce any of the four wives he took between the end of his service in the Civil War and his death in September 1890.[32]

Civil War pension records offer a glimpse into bigamy and what scholar Beverly Schwartzberg terms "fluid marriage" in the nineteenth century. Soldiers and their widows were entitled to a pension from the federal government. Sometimes two or more women would apply for the money citing the same soldier's service. The files collected on these "contested widows" demonstrate that bigamy was "unusual, but not rare." Divorces were difficult to obtain, leaving restless or unhappy spouses with few options other than simply to leave and start over elsewhere. Geographic mobility made re-creating oneself rather simple. Some who fled made up new names for themselves, but many did not feel the need. They just hid their pasts and began again.[33]

None of this seemed untoward for those of limited experience with the law. Many people believed that living with someone made you married, and living apart from someone made you divorced. Others thought that the mere act of filing for divorce ended a marriage, freeing the parties to marry someone new. State judges sometimes encouraged this confusion. In New York, a Judge Rockwell decided that a man living with a woman and calling her his wife was for all legal purposes her husband, even though they were not actually married, and could be prosecuted for bigamy if he married another while she was alive. In another bigamy case, a South Carolina judge said his state had no law "prescribing a marriage ceremonial." Simply taking vows and "going to housekeeping" made a couple legally married in a union "which cannot be annulled, so long as they both do live." Informal marriages, however, could end with equally informal divorces. The true extent of these extralegal arrangements is unknowable.[34]

The bigamy of other Americans does not excuse Conway's deceit and apparent cruelty. He and Cornelia had been married for about fifteen years and had seven children together, five of them surviving, when he married Frances Rankin; the youngest, Edward, was a toddler. Cornelia would have known the Rankin family in Louisville. Matilda owned property on Chestnut Street, near the Barbours, and her sons worked with Conway on the rivers. To Cornelia, Frances may have seemed like a child, which indeed she was when she gave birth to Thomas Conway Rankin. Cornelia's own age as reported in the census varied widely, but she got "younger" after Conway betrayed her. Reporting herself as thirty-eight years old in 1850, she aged only two years by 1860 (forty) and was born even later in the 1870 and 1880 censuses.

Still, it is not clear that Cornelia was aware, at least at first, that her husband, away often on the river, had established a permanent residence in Alton with a new wife and family. Cleveland city directories throughout the 1860s and into the 1870s accurately updated Barbour's business pursuits in Alton, information Cornelia must have received from Conway or their son Joseph, who spent time with his father. A steward in the 1856 directory and a sailor in the 1861 edition, Conway was reported in the 1866–67 Cleveland directory as "Barbour, Conway, restaurant Alton, Ills [*sic*], h 206 Case Ave." The following year, the directory included "Barbour C, agent, h 206 Case," about the same time Conway began selling transit insurance at his Alton restaurant. He was a "hotel keeper" in the 1870–71 directory; in 1872, the directory gave only his street address in Cleveland. Cornelia did not include Conway as a part of the household in the 1870 census, even as she continued to update his occupational adventures to the compilers of the city directory.[35]

Court records suggest a breach and a bizarre collaboration between Conway and Cornelia in 1869, a decade after he married Frances. Back in July 1853, Conway had purchased thirty-one acres of forested land in Lake County, Ohio. In the fall of 1869, probably as a result of financial pressures in Alton, Conway had the acreage transferred into the names of his sons Joseph and Edward. The boys were also given a court-appointed guardian, Cleveland attorney John C. Hutchins, because their father, according to the filing, was dead. The two minors lived with Conway's "divorced wife." Hutchins immediately petitioned the court to allow sale of the property for the support and education of the two children. As a lengthy court case involving the land and its timber wound through the courts, Hutchins covered the cost of shoes and clothing for the boys and also paid their mother for their board. Cornelia would have appreciated the extra cash. Some months earlier, in the spring of 1869, Conway lost the Case Avenue property, and it was sold from beneath her, although the transaction was not finalized until much later. The notion that Conway was dead, although untrue, did not seem to bother her: she reported herself as a widow in the 1873 Cleveland directory. By that time, she was living not in her Case Avenue home but, perhaps fittingly, on Cleveland's Payne Avenue.[36]

Life could not have been easy for Cornelia. Conway and Cornelia's middle daughter, named for her mother, was the only school-aged child in the family not attending classes in 1860 and may have had special needs. Cuyahoga County death records show that young Cornelia died of an unspecified accident on 30 May 1860, at age eight and three months. She was buried in Cleveland's Erie Street Cemetery, and it is unknown whether her father, then living in Alton, attended the burial. Although Cornelia remained in the Case Avenue house for a couple of years after Barbour sold it to his friend Henry Basse of Alton, she reported no property in the 1870 census. Son Joseph helped pay the rent by selling books.[37]

As Conway moved to Alton and beyond, Joseph provided the ongoing link between his parents, and he may have told his mother the truth of the situation, despite remaining close to his father. Just when Cornelia learned of her husband's perfidy remains unclear. That she reported his occupations with updated veracity to compilers of the Cleveland city directory suggests, on the one hand, she was unaware for a time that she had been abandoned. On the other hand, nineteenth-century moral standards leave open the possibility that she knew what was going on but denied it. As Schwartzberg notes, being deserted was cause for shame. It even had its own term: abandoned women were known as "grass widows."[38]

Free black women in the nineteenth century were subject to gender restrictions similar in many ways to those of their white sisters. Women were to be supportive, deferential, domestic, and quiet. Black newspapers, organizational bylaws, and churches reinforced broader societal expectations for both black men and women, while also making adherence to these norms a part of the race struggle. The search for acceptance and respectability in a hostile world meant that transgressions against gender roles became offenses against the progress of the entire community. Black men were to provide for their families by learning a skill, working hard, and personifying strength and sobriety. Black women were to take care of their men, their children, and their homes by being pillars of morality and thrift.[39]

Black gender conventions were not identical to those in white society, however. Black women bore the additional burden of garnering income for black families. They worked in other people's homes or, more preferably, in their own. They also participated in reform efforts in the public sphere and were encouraged, within limits, to do so by black men. Women joined men as delegates to the 1854 emigration convention in Cleveland; one of the female delegates was Delany's wife. Yet black women who criticized black men for not sufficiently defending the race found themselves ostracized. Maria Stewart, a black lecturer in Boston, was forced to leave the city after wondering in a speech if it was blindness, stupidity, or ignorance that kept black men from doing what they should on behalf of their people. Nonetheless, some acceptance by the African American community of female political participation and a general reverence for the education of both sexes meant that black females had some advantages over their white counterparts, although the totality of their personal and societal responsibilities was heavier. African American culture encouraged black female accomplishment. Historian Shirley Carlson Portwood has argued that, in the last decades of the nineteenth century, black women were expected to be both intelligent and feminine, ideals not seen to be in conflict within the African American community.[40]

If by the end of century these differences between white and black gender conventions had widened, free African American women in the middle decades of the nineteenth century, particularly those aspiring to the middle class, knew just as well that respectability in the public eye was to be prized. Perhaps Cornelia knew well and early what had happened with Conway but resolved to maintain a public decorum despite private heartache—to protect appearances for her own sake, in other words. She was a proud woman.

Conway Barbour went to Cleveland to dabble in politics and separate his two women. Apparently uninterested in actually emigrating overseas, Conway, by his participation in Delany's convention, had planted a seed of political ambition that would come to full bloom a few years later. For now, however, he set that aside. On a crisp January morning in 1859, he wed a second woman and commenced a new chapter in his professional adventurism. Using experiences accumulated in Kentucky and Ohio, he began creating his next persona in southwestern Illinois, the civic-minded entrepreneur.

THREE

Alton

THE THREE YEARS between Conway Barbour's move to Cleveland and his marriage to Frances in 1859 were critical in the country's descent into civil war. As Illinois senator Stephen Douglas's theory of popular sovereignty consumed lives and the careers of territorial governors in Kansas, the slaveholding South became increasingly emboldened. After one northern friend of the South, Democrat Franklin Pierce, handed over the White House to another northerner of southern proclivities, Democrat James Buchanan, in March 1857, the national argument over slavery shifted markedly in the southerners' favor. Buchanan used the coercive power of his office to try to force congressional acceptance of a proslavery constitution for Kansas even though Kansans were demonstrably anti-slavery. This enraged members of the newly formed Republican Party and created a rift between the sitting president and his would-be successor, Douglas, architect of the Kansas-Nebraska Act.

The issue of slavery's expansion was ostensibly moot in March after U.S. Supreme Court chief justice Roger Taney declared in the Dred Scott decision that blacks were not national citizens and that any state's recognition of their citizenship held no currency elsewhere in the country. In May, William Walker, the Tennessee filibuster who attempted to make Nicaragua an extension of the slaveholding South, was greeted by 10,000 well-wishers when he fled to New Orleans, an indication of southern support for his venture. By August, a deep economic contraction that hit the North far harder than the South proved to southerners the superiority of their way of life. Their victories accumulated, menacing African Americans.

Illinois' Abraham Lincoln, in his 1858 senatorial debates with Stephen Douglas, offered some hope to the country's blacks. Slavery, Lincoln said, was immoral and should be restricted regardless of the Dred Scott decision. Douglas, clinging to states' rights, had the burden of arguing that popular sovereignty remained viable despite the Supreme Court ruling.

And each time Douglas tried to reassure antislavery northern Democrats, he alienated the southern wing of the party that he needed to get the nomination in 1860. The revelation of northern support for John Brown's 1859 raid on the federal arsenal at Harper's Ferry, Virginia, was the end of any chance for compromise, if one had ever existed, and the beginning of the Confederate Army.[1]

As crisis lay upon crisis, Barbour, the erstwhile emigrationist, was putting down new roots. In March 1859, two months after his marriage to Frances, Barbour bought a one-acre lot in Alton's Mounier subdivision for $1,000. Under the terms of the contract, he put $200 down and then paid installments of $267 at six-, twelve-, and eighteen-month intervals, at 6 percent interest. The property was paid and the deed released 1 July 1861. This was home to his growing family. In 1862, baby Julia joined Thomas and Fannie. The land purchase made the Barbours members of the small African American community in Alton.

Like Louisville and Cleveland, Alton was a water town. For a time in the early nineteenth century, the city vied with St. Louis for population and commercial dominance on its part of the Mississippi River. That competition came to a quick and bloody close in 1837, when Alton elites sanctioned and participated in the murder of abolitionist newspaper editor Elijah Lovejoy. Dr. Horace Beal, one of three city doctors involved in the killing, reportedly "danced a little jig ahead of the horse" carrying the dead editor to his home. The doctor "pretended to be playing an instrument" and announced to passersby that he would play a fife if he had one. The lawlessness, compounded by the Panic of 1837 and the related inability of the state legislature to deliver transportation improvements, destroyed Alton's budding reputation. Property values plummeted, and some of the murderers, all of whom escaped punishment, left town after the economic consequences of their actions stirred belated indignation in the community.[2]

The events of 1837 must have had a chilling effect on the city's small African American population, particularly since the crime took place in open view, involved leaders of the white community, and the culprits were found not guilty by the court. The black community in Madison County was very small, between 2 percent and 3 percent, until the war years, when it doubled to around 5 percent. In the 1845 state census, the greater Alton area was home to approximately half of the county's 432 African Americans. Ten were listed in the census as indentured or as "French Negroes," slaves grandfathered under the state constitution of 1818.

In proportion to the white population, blacks were more demographically significant in Foster and Pin Oak Townships, even though their absolute numbers were small. The Pin Oak enclave was historically significant as well. In 1819, Edward Coles, who later became governor, freed his slaves and helped them claim federal plots in the hinterland. In this wilderness, a small African American community took shape, families who would send their sons to fight, and in some cases die, in the Civil War many years later. An 1851 county map refers to that part of Pin Oak Township as the "Negro Settlement."[3]

When that map was drawn, the number of blacks had grown to 449, or 2.2 percent of the county population. A decade later, Barbour and his family were among the county's 562 people of color, about 1.8 percent of the total population. By the 1865 state census, more than 2,100 blacks (5 percent) lived among a total county population of about 42,000. The wartime influx of runaways and freedmen was unwelcome to many whites, and the percentage of the black population in Madison County remained relatively flat over the next two decades. Whereas Alton had been home to about half of the African American population in the county in 1845, it was home to about a quarter of the county's blacks twenty years later. The newer residents settled in the townships surrounding Alton and in more distant areas of the county, seeking, perhaps, to remain out of view.[4]

As Alton-area blacks made small but perceptible economic gains in the years before the war, they also responded to their deteriorating social and legal position. In 1853, sixteen years after Lovejoy's murder cast a shadow over the city, Alton again made national headlines, this time in a case stemming from the Fugitive Slave Act enacted as part of the Compromise of 1850. A white man from Memphis, J. T. Leath, brought a mulatto girl, Amanda Kitchell, seventeen, to Alton in 1851, ostensibly with the object of setting her free. She lived with an aunt in Alton until marrying a boatman her same age, Alfred Chavis, in late 1852. Less than a month after the marriage, in January 1853, five men broke into the Chavis home, grabbed Amanda, and took her to Levi Davis, the U.S. commissioner charged with enforcing the Fugitive Slave Act. One of the attackers, Malcolm McCullom, produced a bill of sale from Leath's father as well as witnesses from both Memphis and Alton. Davis had no choice under the law but to decide for the plaintiff.

Citizens of Alton, both black and white, were outraged. They raised the $1,200 McCullom demanded for the woman, even though some of the city's abolitionists balked at being involved in the traffic of human beings.

Amanda's husband mortgaged the home he owned with his mother, Eliza-beth, and other members of the community did the same. Black merchant Cyrus Howard was one of several people who borrowed against their property. Howard wrote to the *National Era* with details of the events and said he could no longer afford to buy the newspaper because of his new debt. The sale price provided a nice profit for McCullom, who, according to his bill of sale, had paid $400 for Amanda. A disgusted Judge Davis resigned his position, unwilling to participate further in the enforcement of the law, and a county history suggests that whites believed themselves washed of the Lovejoy murder by their support of Amanda Chavis.[5]

Alton's African Americans would have disagreed, especially since Illinois' black laws were more likely to affect them than their counter-parts in the rural areas. As in Ohio, the Northwest Ordinance of 1787 was supposed to prohibit slavery in the Illinois country, which had been introduced by the French in 1719 and continued when the region came under English control after the Seven Years' War. Delegates to the state's constitutional convention in 1818 attempted to sidestep the ordinance by inserting the word *hereafter* in the clause on slavery or involuntary ser-vitude in Illinois; that is to say the convention construed the Northwest Ordinance as forbidding only *new* slaves, an interpretation invoked by some in Ohio years earlier. The constitution also codified territorial-era circumventions that sanctioned voluntary servitude of those already in the state, including the French Negroes. Because of these actions, Illinois had more slaves than any other purportedly free state.[6]

Whereas civil rights for African Americans were a contentious issue in the deliberations of the Ohio constitutional convention, delegates to the Illinois convention did not bother themselves with defining a role for free blacks. The legislature took that up the following year, constructing the state's first comprehensive black code. Illinois law ostensibly barred African Americans from taking up residency in the state, and, as in Ohio, blacks were required to register and post assurance with the county on arrival. And, as in Ohio, the law was haphazardly enforced: Barbour and his family are not registered in any of Madison County's "Negro Books." State law denied the vote, court standing, and equal access to education, among other provisions.

The legislature elaborated the black laws over time, even as it rejected petitions to repeal the entire code. A state senate judiciary committee report in 1847 refused to repeal the laws differentiating blacks from whites, saying that "no acts of legislation will or can ever raise the African in this country above the level" he then held. Any black man unhappy with

Illinois' statutes could go to Africa, the report said, and there "test the powers of his mind for self-government." The judiciary committee report commented that the Illinois House of Representatives had rejected a similar petition the previous year, and the matter had been put "forever at rest." Further, the report said that whites signing such petitions were foolish in seeking redress of grievances *not their own* and that blacks should disabuse themselves of the idea that such requests would ever be granted. Illinois legislators were some of the most obstinate in the Old Northwest. All of the state's black laws were in place until after the Civil War.[7]

Judging by the transcripts of a "colored" citizens' convention held in Alton in 1856, Alton's African American leadership, while resenting the black laws, may have been less confrontational than were others in the state. Mindful, possibly, of their small numbers and precarious standing, Alton blacks supported *requesting* rather than *demanding* their rights. At the Convention of the Colored Citizens of the State of Illinois held in the city in November 1856, they argued for moderating the language adopted but failed by one vote to win the point.

Seventeen delegates attended the Alton convention; eight were local men, most of whom were middle class. Isaac Kelly was born a slave in Georgia but was freed at age twenty-one and sent to Alton to be educated at Shurtleff College. Major Charles Hunter, a prominent white land developer active in the Underground Railroad, became Kelly's guardian. Kelly, a subconductor on the North Star route, was a barber and owned a public bathhouse. He had once lived with Reverend R. J. Robinson, a grocery merchant born in Virginia. Both men were active in the city's Union Baptist Church, where Robinson was pastor until 1866. Cyrus "C. C." Richardson was a Kentucky-born blacksmith; H. D. King, a grocer. The other local delegates were Louis Overton of Wood River Township; Edward "Dempy" White, a barber and cook from Ohio; Emmanuel Wilkerson, a Tennessee-born laborer; and James H. Johnson, a farmer in Foster Township. These men were neither the wealthiest nor the poorest of the county's black men, although their holdings were at least twice the average per household in the Alton area. Some, like Kelly and Robinson, were well known throughout the city when the convention met and for decades afterward.[8]

The convention's Cook County contingent was at the forefront of the effort to eradicate Illinois' black laws. John Jones was the most prominent black leader in the cause. Born free in North Carolina, he and his wife arrived in Alton in 1844 seeking the presumed advantages of life in a free state. Like John Malvin in Ohio, however, Jones found himself subject to unexpected restrictions. As required, he and his wife, Mary Jane, registered with the Madison County clerk. Although Jones told the convention how much he loved Alton, where "I first breathed free air," he soon left for Chicago, where he made a small fortune as a tailor and involved himself in race politics, gaining prominence as vice president of the National Convention of Black Freemen in Cleveland in 1848. Jones, who thought Delany's emigration plans misguided, was accompanied in Alton by H. Ford Douglas, a delegate to the 1854 convention. A "Mass Meeting of Colored Citizens of Chicago," in August 1856, complained specifically about the denial of suffrage, equal standing in the courts, and access to public schools. The purpose of the Alton meeting three months later was to develop a plan for putting these issues before the public and keeping them there, to "give our Legislature no rest."[9]

At Alton, the delegates resolved to organize a repeal association whose aim was to seek relief from the black laws. Toward that end, the group said it would raise a contingent fund, organize local and regional meetings, circulate petitions, and collect data on the condition of blacks in the state. While the nine resolves in the Declaration of Sentiment and Plan of Action were readily approved, the convention split over language in its preamble, with Madison County's delegates leading the call for a milder tone. As Barbour drifted away from emigration as the solution for free blacks in Ohio and elsewhere, the freemen meeting in Alton wrestled with how to end their oppression in Illinois.

The preamble promised that blacks would act in their own interest, "neither asking nor giving quarter, spurning all compromises." Reverend Robinson objected, saying the words "savored of braggadocio." Alton's Louis Overton pointed to the Missouri Compromise as evidence that compromise was "a good thing." Their fellow Altonian, grocer H. D. King, however, had no quarrel with the language. He "wanted . . . to assert his manhood for *once*." When the language came to a vote, four of the seven delegates voting to delete it were from Alton; two local men voted against the deletion. Two more Alton blacks were absent or did not vote, but one of them, Richardson, John Jones's brother-in-law, had said previously that the language was too harsh. It was a minority sentiment, however, and the controversial phraseology remained in the preamble.[10]

The debate suggests that Altonians participating in the convention were interested in excising the black laws from Illinois' books but were perhaps more pragmatic about methods. If so, their caution went unheeded by their friends and unrewarded by their neighbors. In 1862, even as they sent their sons to fight in the Civil War, Illinois voters rejected a proposal that would have modified the state's residency restrictions on blacks. Thus, given an opportunity to strike a blow for liberty and some measure of equality, about 58 percent of Illinois voters responded in the negative. Only the conclusion of the war and the constitutional amendments enacted therewith brought relief for Illinois blacks.[11]

Conway Barbour, on his arrival in Alton in late 1858, found a progressive and successful African American community striving for and obtaining some measure of economic advancement, cautiously pursuing civil rights, and seeking self-improvement. The editors of the *Alton Weekly Courier* were amazed at the quality of the pupils at the "new colored school" they visited in a church basement in 1858. Teacher John Robinson, the Baptist minister's son, was doing a fine job. The students' academic performance was first rate, but the editors were particularly impressed with the children's singing, noting that "possession of superior voice is a characteristic of the African race," an indication of the editors' stereotypical view of African Americans. The paper also praised the formation in February 1859 of a Sons of Temperance group by the city's black men. C. C. Richardson was "Chief Guardian" and Reverend Robinson the "Recruiting Scribe" in the new organization. Alfred Chavis, whose wife had been abducted by slave catchers in 1853, was elected "shepherd." Although the paper reported a month later that membership had already doubled, it is unlikely that Barbour, the steamboat steward, joined this organization.[12]

Barbour became a property-owning member of Alton's African American community even as the white community was in turmoil. Only a couple of months before he and Frances were married in the city, Alton hosted the final Lincoln-Douglas debate. More than six thousand people gathered around a platform erected near city hall on 15 October 1858 to hear the two "gladiators close . . . with each other for the last time." Banners were prohibited near the dais, but the city streets were decorated with partisan slogans and poems: "Old Abe and Free Labor" countered by "State Sovereignty–National Unity." Local dignitaries feted the candidates before the event at their respective hotels, Lincoln at the Franklin House and Douglas at the Alton House.[13]

Douglas, who spoke first and finally, brutalized the Buchanan administration so intensely that Lincoln had only to acknowledge his opponent's points to make his own—at first. Overall, however, the debate reduced itself to Douglas's defense of popular sovereignty and Lincoln's position that the Dred Scott decision left the concept as insubstantial as a soup made with "the shadow of a pigeon that had been starved to death." Despite the *Alton Weekly Courier*'s declaration that Lincoln triumphed and Douglas dodged, the crowd was reportedly overwhelmingly pro-Douglas. Madison County had three members in the Illinois General Assembly, and Douglas got the votes of all three. He went to the U.S. Senate, but Lincoln achieved a national reputation. Two years later, as the Barbours were settling into their new home, the crucial issues argued in the debate produced national crisis and the Civil War.[14]

Alton's strategic location assured it a vital role in the Union war effort, although a large portion of the populace was sympathetic to the South. As demonstrated in the 1858 vote, Madison County's white voters were not fully supportive of Lincoln's Free-Soil position on the extension of slavery. Lincoln won the county in 1860 but by a thin sixty-one-vote margin. Southern by geography, heritage, and tradition, Madison County whites were generally of one mind on the inferiority of black people but were bitterly divided on the issues of slavery and federal authority. Judging by their voting record, about half of the voters in the county believed that the same states' right doctrine that allowed them to emasculate blacks as political beings also allowed southern states to regard African Americans as property. For those voters, southerners' ability to enslave blacks was inextricably linked to their own ability to legislate dominance over the black minority and achieve economic security.[15]

After Fort Sumter and Lincoln's call for volunteers, Alton teemed with activity. It became an important base for the gathering and transshipment of troops, and its prison became an unhappy destination for captured Confederates and Union men awaiting parole. When Union general Nathaniel Lyon seized a cache of arms from the U.S. arsenal in St. Louis in early 1861, a steamer carried them to the Alton levee to be loaded on the rails for Springfield. Reports of prisoner transfers back and forth between St. Louis and the Alton prison peppered the pages of the *Alton Telegraph* as did stories of escapes, executions, and street violence often associated with off-duty soldiers. So frenetic and overwhelming was the amount of news in the first months of the war that the weekly paper went daily to try to keep up.[16]

The *Telegraph* was Unionist and engaged in an ongoing editorial battle with its counterpart, the *Alton Democrat*, although partisans of the latter usually won at the polls. For example, the *Telegraph* promoted a Union ticket of loyal men, Republican or Democrat, when elections came around in late 1861, but the ticket lost to the Democrats. Although the paper urged voters in 1862 to reject a new state constitution it thought too laden with expense and new offices, both the city and the county voted for it. The *Telegraph* favored the use of contrabands by the Union Army as a smart war measure but said emancipation of all slaves could be dealt with later, after the war was won. On the issue of the black laws, a separate vote in 1862, the paper was silent. Blasted by the *Alton Democrat* as being pro-black, the *Telegraph* countered that the war was about slavery, not blacks. The planter class of the South, the paper said, would enslave whites if it could.[17]

Although the *Telegraph* did not advocate civil rights for blacks, it mocked a city attorney who threatened free blacks in May 1861. The influx of blacks in the first flush of the war prompted Alton's prosecuting attorney, James W. Davis, to warn recent arrivals to the city that they had thirty days to leave or be prosecuted. Heavy fines would be levied against them, and those unable to pay would be offered at public auction, in accordance with the law. Railroad companies and steamboat operators in particular were warned about bringing free blacks to the city.[18]

The *Telegraph*'s lengthy response to Davis's warning was thick with sarcasm as it belittled Davis and revealed its vision of what constituted acceptable black behavior. The paper hoped that Davis's exertions against free blacks would not deter him from his other official duties, even though it was very important that blacks guilty of "so *atrocious* a crime as being free should be attended to." Although Alton's blacks were "among the most quiet, orderly, law-abiding and sober of our population," their "freedom in a *free country* is too gross an offense to pass unnoticed." The editors urged the public not to find fault with this "faithful servant" but to be sure to support him "for any place he may ask" in the future. The attack on Davis, then, incorporated the notion that Alton's free blacks deserved defending because they were quiet and did not bother anyone; that is, they were "good."[19]

No Alton blacks were subjected to Davis's penalties, although, according to William Wells Brown, six blacks in Hancock County, in western Illinois, were auctioned off in lieu of fines in February 1863. Still, the threat alone would have been enough to frighten Alton's black community. And they would surely have noticed that Alton's city council refused until December 1863 to fly the American flag on the spire atop city hall, a clear signal of its sympathies. The council acquiesced just as the state began organizing its first regiment of black soldiers, the Twenty-Ninth United States Colored Infantry.[20]

Northern blacks attempting to enlist in the army at the outbreak of the Civil War were turned away, and even antislavery publications insisted that it was to be a white man's war. By 1862, however, the desire to deprive the rebels of their slaves and the need for manpower prompted Congress to pass the Second Confiscation Act and the Militia Act, both allowing enrollment of African Americans in the war effort, ostensibly as laborers. After the Emancipation Proclamation, effective 1 January 1863, opened up the possibility of using blacks as soldiers, recruitment began in earnest. Eastern states obtained federal permission to solicit Illinois blacks with patriotic language and large bounties. Rhode Island's generous and aggressive recruiting efforts were a concern to Illinois governor Richard Yates, who sought and received federal permission to raise a regiment of black troops to help fill the state's quota. The First Illinois became the Twenty-Ninth United States Colored Infantry when it mustered in at Quincy in April 1864. Company E was raised in Madison County.[21]

─────

By early 1863, Conway Barbour was looking for opportunities off the river, and the organization of black regiments in Illinois gave him an idea. Recognizing this new possibility, he boldly approached the Illinois governor directly. In a letter dated 3 February 1863, Barbour wrote Yates that he had seen a poster announcing the formation of black regiments. "I'am at your servis as a recruiting officer," Barbour wrote, "or will raise a company to comand." A man who had previously toyed with the notion that blacks could only achieve their rights by leaving the United States then bragged, "I under stand how to get to patriotism free or conterbands," and offered to travel throughout the state or interior to solicit volunteers. "I'am sure they will fight like tigers," Barbour wrote. He also called the governor's attention to "one thing more." The governor should make certain the black soldiers had leaders known to favor their enrollment in the service: "Then the[y] will be lead to battle and not to slaughter." He said he wanted to lead a regiment or a brigade and would "charge on rebels no matter ware." If his offer met with the governor's approval, "pleas inform me and tell me that I shall led." He would await an answer. However, he wrote that if the answer was no, he asked that his name not be made public. He signed the letter "Conway Barbour, a free man."[22]

Here we have Barbour in his own voice. He wanted to be a leader of men and offered to travel anywhere in order to achieve his goal. Although he spoke of patriotism and rebels, he did not mention slavery or slaves. Still, his racial pride was apparent. The blacks would "fight like tigers." His admonition to Yates that black soldiers should be led to battle and not to slaughter demonstrated an understanding of the racial politics of the war and a healthy fear that the use of black troops could mean the sacrifice of black men by pro-Union, but racist, whites—a breed with which he was familiar in Alton.

Most striking is what the letter indicates about Barbour's self-concept. Approximately age forty-three at the time, Barbour might have simply joined the army, but he did not want to serve as much as he wanted to lead—"tell me that I shall led"—phraseology that reveals his intense ambition, even hubris. Barbour's self-importance was such that he anticipated a public response to his letter from the state governor, and he did not want to be publicly humiliated by a negative answer. Furthermore, he wanted to make sure that the governor knew he was a free man, distinguished from the contrabands he said he could bring to the cause. Beyond its content, the letter reveals a simple literacy and begs the question of how he acquired it. Perhaps, as historian Thomas Buchanan has suggested, the riverboats in the South functioned, in part, as illicit schoolhouses where slaves and free blacks acquired a rudimentary education.[23]

When Yates did not respond, Barbour wrote again on 28 February 1863, reminding the governor that he was "wateing for the worde." He told Yates he was not afraid to fight, even though "fighting means kill som person or get killed trying to save your countery." It did not matter to him where he was killed, he said, if that were to be his fate. He implied that Yates's failed to reply to his first letter out of political caution. "If the fear of copperheads is to stop the raising [of] tropes[,] the[y] will be doing all the rebells wish them to do," Barbour wrote. He said he had visited St. Louis three times since his first letter and found a good many men who would enlist in Illinois because "your kindeness to your troops at Shilo is well remembered by colord men."

Having both rather insulted and then flattered the state's chief executive, Barbour got to the point. He had been "stewarding the river" from Louisville and St. Louis to New Orleans for sixteen years, ever since around the time Robert Bell bought an insurance policy on him in the late

1840s. It was, he said, his business. While waiting to go into the army, he had "refused 2 situations" of employment. He wanted to know if he was waiting in vain because, if so, he needed to get back on the river. And then he tried one last flourish. "My Liberty is as sweet as any mans on Earth and my Life is no passenger. Ples answer," he wrote. Not just along for the ride—an apt metaphor for a riverman—he was willing to sacrifice his sweet freedom for his country.[24]

The Yates administration did not reply publicly or otherwise to either letter. Apparently unaware that black troops were to have white officers, Barbour would not have been allowed to command. He might have been appointed a recruiter, as were Martin Delany, H. Ford Douglas, John Mercer Langston, and others, but that did not happen. Illinois officials neither acknowledged nor accepted Barbour's offer, even as recruitment for the Twenty-Ninth United States Colored Infantry and other black regiments proceeded.

His military ambitions thwarted, Barbour reassessed his options. Work on the rivers had provided his livelihood since the 1840s, and steamboats remained vital to the economy and the war effort. However, a transition to rail transportation, which started before the war, continued apace. Alton had been promised major transportation improvements by the state legislature in the late 1830s, but that commitment was undermined, as we have seen, by Alton's damaged reputation after the Lovejoy murder and by the general economic contraction of the Van Buren years. By the mid-1840s, however, railroad construction resumed. The Alton and Sangamon line was chartered in 1847 to connect the river city with the state capital and was finished in 1852. Unable to complete the full run to St. Louis, the rail line purchased steamboats to get passengers and freight to Missouri. As the Civil War commenced, the rail lines pushed through to East St. Louis. By 1864, a reconstituted Chicago and Alton Railroad took freight and passengers directly to East St. Louis, decreasing the profitability of the steamboats.[25]

Barbour may not have understood the diminishing viability of the steamboats, but he could see the number of soldiers and businessmen filtering through Alton during the Civil War, all needing food and a clean bed. An experienced steward and cook on the steamboats, Barbour hired on at the Mercantile Restaurant on Belle Street in late 1863. The Mercantile was owned by a German émigré, Henry Basse, a miller by trade and an active player in Alton-area real estate dealings. Madison County deed records show Basse buying and selling properties throughout the 1860s and after, often at an enormous profit. Barbour and Basse were business partners during the 1860s, although the nature of the partnership is murky. Basse was an executor of Barbour's mother-in-law's estate four years after Conway's death, suggesting that Basse was a friend of the family, not its abuser. In fact, the evidence indicates that Basse was the financier of virtually all Conway's business ventures in Alton and that he lost a lot of money in the process.

Basse's willingness to back Barbour was fortuitous. In 1863, there were only two lenders in Alton, the Alton Bank and the banking arm of the Alton Mutual Insurance and Savings Company. Neither might have been disposed to help Barbour, an African American with a relatively short history in town. As John Sibley Butler has written, blacks have found it difficult to borrow money to start businesses throughout American history. Probate records and other sources suggest that "banking" often consisted simply of promissory notes arranged between friends and neighbors, black and white. Men with money lent it to those who had none. William Johnson, a wealthy black barber in Natchez, kept track of his accounts in his diary. Probate records for Henry Blair, a rich black farmer who lived near Barbour in Madison County, reveal dozens of loans to other men (and one woman), ranging from as little as $25 to almost $1,500. Two banks opened in the summer of 1865, the Alton National Bank, a reorganized version of the Alton Bank, and the First National Bank of Alton, but Barbour continued to do business with his friend. Their personal relationship made his businesses possible.[26]

Basse began advertising the Mercantile Restaurant, also known as the Mercantile Saloon, in the *Alton Telegraph* in October 1863 as "now open" and offering meals at all hours on short notice. Two months later, Barbour purchased Basse's lease interest in the restaurant and its contents on a promissory note for $900 due in two years at 6 percent interest. Barbour's career as an independent businessman in Alton was under way, although the first advertisement with his name on it did not appear until February 1865. In the advertisement for the Mercantile Saloon, "C. Barbour, Prop." announced, "I constantly keep on hand the various kinds of game and fish of the season which are to be had in this or the St. Louis market. Meals at all hours. Table wines of all varieties. Prices Liberal. Board by the day or week." A billiard room with four tables was adjacent to the dining room.[27]

Between Barbour's purchase of the lease in December 1863 and his first advertisement in early 1865, several other transactions had taken place. In July 1864, Barbour sold the Mounier property, purchased shortly after his marriage, to Basse for $2,500. An unspecified encumbrance to

Ebenezer Marsh, a trustee, was quitclaimed to facilitate the sale. The selling price represented a huge profit over the $1,000 Barbour had paid for the property and might have covered the note Barbour owed Basse for the Mercantile, although Madison County records do not show that the Mercantile note was ever paid in full. In October 1864, Barbour purchased two lots in the Mechanic's Square section of Alton for $1,200 in cash. This was now his family's home.[28]

The economic viability of Barbour's Mercantile Restaurant and its billiards room seems to have been solid. According to the 1865 Illinois census, the Mercantile was home to nine white males and seven black males, a total of sixteen men. As the mortgage to Basse included only eight mattresses, the Mercantile was apparently full, depending on the number of shared beds. The hotel and restaurant was also a favorite of the *Telegraph*, which flattered Barbour by comparing the Mercantile to a well-known establishment in the state capital. The newspaper's praise, however, must be filtered through its concern for its own profit. The hard line between editorial content and advertisements demanded by journalists and expected by readers today did not exist in nineteenth-century newspapers, as editors regularly invited their readers to patronize individuals and companies advertising in the same edition. Even so, the support lavished upon Barbour in the *Telegraph* was exceptional.[29]

A front-page article on 10 February 1865 declared,

> Barbour's Mercantile Saloon is an institution in our city. Coming here when there was nothing of the kind in Alton, Mr. Barbour has the satisfaction of knowing that he is the only one who has ever engaged in the business here and made it pay sufficiently well to continue. We know by the best evidence that he keeps all the luxuries and game of the season, and often calls upon the market of St. Louis to supply his larder. The Mercantile Saloon is to Alton what Doul's is to Springfield. Give Barbour a call.[30]

Edward (Emil) Doul was a French saloonkeeper in the capital city. In the 1860 census, he had $8,000 in real estate and $2,000 in personal property and would soon own much more. Barbour could only dream of such wealth, but the recognition of his business savvy was more gratifying. Barbour had a paid advertisement in the same issue and continued to advertise liberally in the paper throughout his years in Alton. The paper's promotion of Barbour's Mercantile as the best guesthouse south of

Springfield might have constituted crony capitalism, an honest appraisal, or some admixture of the two.[31]

Barbour's confreres in the black business community did not receive this level of support, even though they also advertised in the *Telegraph*, suggesting that Barbour enjoyed a special status with the newspaper's editors. Isaac Kelly frequently advertised the "City Baths" adjoining his barbershop as of 1861, and H. D. King consistently advertised his grocery store. Neither was singled out for editorial praise in the *Telegraph*, even though King worked with Barbour at the Mercantile.[32]

The Mercantile was a small boardinghouse, limiting Barbour's prospects. He continued to advertise through the spring of 1865, but in May he announced the sale of the business to "J. Williams," possibly John Williams, son of the owner of the Piasa House, another local hotel. In an advertisement, Barbour thanked the community for its liberal patronage over the previous few years; Williams promised to merit continued support and said King would remain with him at the Mercantile. No mortgage arrangement between Barbour and Williams exists in Madison County deed records, and so the selling price of the Mercantile is unknown. Shortly before this sale, in late April 1865, Cleveland attorney J. E. Ingersoll, who held in trust the title to Barbour's Case Avenue property, transferred ownership back to Barbour for $1. The Cuyahoga County recorder of deeds left no record of Barbour putting the property in Ingersoll's care. Perhaps Barbour put the property in Ingersoll's name temporarily to shield it from creditors in case the Mercantile failed. Cornelia and her children still lived on the homestead, and, as noted, it is not clear when Cornelia became aware of Conway's new family in Alton. Trying to protect her, himself, or both, Barbour retrieved the asset to have at his disposal as he gave up the Mercantile and planned his next move. In November 1865, some months after he announced the sale of the Mercantile, Barbour mortgaged his home in Mechanic's Square to Basse for $1,000 cash, indicating that he was raising money to launch his next, larger hotel and restaurant, the Fifth Avenue Hall.[33]

The timing was inauspicious for business expansion, although Barbour could not have known that. Alton was a lively place during the Civil War. Home to a military post and prison, the city benefited economically from the war. Its flour mills, stone quarries, brick manufactories, and warehouses flourished. Its hotels and boardinghouses were full, its restaurants overflowing with soldiers and businessmen. But when the war ended in the spring of 1865, the soldiers went home. The number of federal military prisoners dropped from 3,000 to 853 by the first of May and to zero by the end of June as men took their oaths and were released or transferred. Peace devastated the economy. According to a county history, the end of the war ushered in a "slump in . . . prosperity that lasted over 15 years. Times were so dull that real estate could hardly be given away." Barbour, with an expanding household of young mouths to feed—a son, Conway Jr., was born in 1865—opened his new business just as hard times were setting in, hard times that would linger for more than a decade.[34]

Even so, Barbour's new Fifth Avenue Hall enjoyed the same warm embrace by the *Telegraph* as had the Mercantile. In March 1866, the paper gave its readers notice of "A Good House." It had learned that Barbour, "so popular as a caterer to the public taste" at the Mercantile, was retrofitting the Valley House. The completed project would feature new bedding and spring mattresses, with "everything . . . kept strictly in number one style." About a month later, an advertisement announced the opening of the Fifth Avenue Hall featuring "every luxury in season and out of season that can be found between New York and New Orleans." Barbour advertised himself as having "30 years' experience as Steward on first class steamboats, and in hotels" and promised "meals prepared and served in from three to five minutes after the order is given." A reading room offered a number of daily papers; ladies were urged to use the parlor instead of the sitting room. The advertisement was signed "C. Barbour, Prop'r."[35]

Barbour was trying to take his business to a new level. He now promised to fill his larder, not just from Alton, St. Louis, and Chicago, but to bring in the best of the season from New York to New Orleans. His assertion of thirty years' experience on the steamboats—he had told Governor Yates sixteen years in 1863—was clearly a marketing ploy, but it also demonstrates pride in his work. The differentiation for ladies—who were invited to sit somewhere other than where men would sit—indicates that he understood gender roles deemed appropriate in the nineteenth century. Overall, one is struck by how upscale Barbour sought to be.

In addition to expanding his business, Barbour returned to politics. In January 1866, he and his friend Edward "Dempy" White sponsored a visit to Alton by John Mercer Langston and James Milton Turner. Barbour knew Langston from the emigration convention in Cleveland and probably knew Turner from his visits to St. Louis. In late 1865, Turner, secretary of the Missouri Equal Rights League, had engaged Langston, president of the National Equal Rights League, to tour Missouri speaking on behalf of black suffrage and access to education. Langston culminated this "Equality Before the Law" campaign with a speech before the Missouri legislature on 9 January 1866; he spoke at city hall in Alton on 1 February and then headed home to Ohio. The event was reported as a great success.[36]

An old customer provided Barbour with more free publicity. William Dowdall, formerly of Alton, was now editor of the *Peoria National Democrat*. He wrote to the *Telegraph* after learning of Barbour's new place. His letter said,

> No man more thoroughly appreciates printers' ink than Mr. Barbour, and no one knows better how to get up a table to please the epicure than he. We speak by the card, having boarded at his table twelve months when proprietor of the Mercantile, and always finding his bills of fare containing everything the market afforded, and done in a style equaled by few and surpassed by none, and now that his rooms are more roomy, elegant, and convenient, he is bound to succeed.[37]

Dowdall's comments, although intended to be complimentary, raise the question of Barbour's solvency. It is clear that Barbour was a self-promoter and appreciated printer's ink. He consistently advertised in the *Telegraph*. But Dowdall's last comment implies that Barbour had not succeeded at the Mercantile and now had a chance to do so. Madison County has no tax records that might illuminate the situation, and, although Barbour's name is indexed in R. G. Dun & Co. records, that is his only mention.

Deed records show that the same day Dowdall's comments and Barbour's first ad appeared in the *Telegraph*, Barbour mortgaged the contents of the Fifth Avenue Hall to Basse. He owed his financier $1,000, due 30 March 1867, for sixteen bedsteads; bedding; dining room, kitchen, and other furniture; and accoutrements. Shortly before the note was due, in January 1867, Barbour quitclaimed his home, which he had sold to Basse in November 1865, to Frances and their children. A month later, Basse quitclaimed the Mechanic's Square lots back to Conway. Barbour had apparently repurchased his home from Basse but still owed the note on the contents of the Fifth Avenue Hall. This sort of financial juggling was the hallmark of Barbour's business dealings but not necessarily unusual in nineteenth-century America or beyond.[38]

The first advertisement for the Fifth Avenue Hall appeared in April 1867, although the hall had apparently been open for some time. An Alton City directory published the previous year listed Barbour as proprietor of the Fifth Avenue Hall, with his son Joseph and Clark Barbour's son Richard among the residents. Again, Conway touted "every luxury" served minutes from order and a separate room for ladies. The advertisement also shows he was now an agent for the Western Transit Insurance Company of St. Louis. A month later, Barbour again mortgaged the contents of the Fifth Avenue Hall to Basse, this time for $2,000 due 1 May 1869. The same sixteen bedsteads, bedding, and other furniture he previously mortgaged for $1,000 now cost twice that amount. He may have been falling deeper into debt, but he may have been raising money for his largest—and last— business enterprise in Alton, in the city's Union Railroad Depot.[39]

The Union Depot was the main city station for the Chicago and Alton Railroad, and it was brand new. The city council granted land on Front Street and Market on the levee in July 1864 for its construction. The exterior of the building, designed to look like a train engine, was completed in July 1867. A September 1867 notice in the *Telegraph* announced, "trains on the Chicago road will stop at the Union Hotel in this city for meals on or after the 23rd inst. [of this month.] Mr. Barbour will need more room for his stylish establishment."[40]

The contents of the Union Hotel were markedly more expensive than those of the Fifth Avenue Hall. In October 1867, Barbour again mortgaged the contents of his business, and again the lender was Basse. The furnishings and supplies included twenty walnut bedsteads, five bureaus, silver-plated serving items, Brussels carpets, $1,000 worth of wine and liquors, two thousand cigars, five barrels of nuts, and more. Barbour owed Basse $5,000 due 13 October 1869. This represented a huge economic investment for the former steamboat steward. He decreased his liabilities by selling the contents of the Fifth Avenue Hall, but for only $370, and that in installments.[41]

Barbour advertised the Union Hotel in the *Telegraph* at least twice a week, beginning in January 1868. Barbour also kept his hand in politics, participating as one of two speakers at a "colored" celebration of the anniversary of the Emancipation Proclamation in January. The next month he spoke at the celebration by the "colored citizens of Alton" of the repeal of the state's black laws.[42]

In March, Barbour contracted with the Alton & St. Louis Packet Company to provide "restaurant style" meals on the company's new steamer, *Belle of Alton*. He hired "celebrated cook and steward Nelson Nicholas" to take charge, but he promised his personal attention as well. He received a glowing notice in the *Telegraph* after the boat's first run. The article said meals were served "in sumptuous style" by the "experienced caterer, Mr. C. Barbour of this city." More importantly, the meals were served on call, an arrangement called "entirely new and destined to be universally popular."[43]

Traditionally, meals on steamboats were included in the price of the ticket and served as a smorgasbord or family-style, in which a variety of dishes were placed on the table and patrons took portions from them. The local paper credited Barbour with inventing the so-called European, or restaurant, system whereby meals were not included in the cost of the ticket but were served and billed as ordered. Declining revenues in the postwar era prompted steamboat owners to economize, producing a "flurry of interest in the restaurant system in 1868 when it was tried on a number of steamboats." Steamboat historian Louis Hunter cited several newspaper articles on the subject, most from Louisville papers. As the earliest of those articles was published 3 June 1868, and Barbour received his praise in May, he may have been among the first to try the restaurant system, demonstrating knowledge of his field and a willingness to break new ground. Unfortunately for Barbour, the practice did not become universally popular and quickly lost favor.[44]

His luck was not any better on land. In 1868, the Chicago and Alton Railroad became the first railroad to put on dining cars. Passengers arriving at the Union Depot, having eaten on the train, had little reason to tarry at the Union Hotel for a meal in the hotel's restaurant. The Union's twenty walnut bedsteads were also unoccupied. The 1868–69 Alton City directory, while praising the establishment as a "good house and well kept," showed that, besides Barbour's son Joseph, only one person boarded at the Union, E. Pfeiffer of Weil & Pfeiffer. Barbour had eight employees, all "colored," but not enough business to support them. By contrast, in the same directory, the Alton House had thirteen employees, excluding the white owner, and forty-eight boarders; the Franklin House had five employees, excluding its white owner, and twenty-three boarders. The reportedly successful and popular caterer was up against the due date on his $5,000 debt to Basse, and the Union Hotel was failing. Under the gun, Barbour, in April 1868, sold all of his Cleveland property to Basse for $3,000, a down payment on his enormous debt to the German miller. Unfortunately, Barbour no longer owned the property free and clear. Basse paid William Williams of Cleveland $400 in June 1868 for a claim against two of the five lots on Case Avenue. Several months later, in February 1869, William Hewitt of Cleveland sued Barbour, Basse, and Cornelia, whose name was not on the property, for $402 owed on two other lots. When payment was not forthcoming, an Ohio Court of Common Pleas ordered a public auction, which took place 7 March 1870. Basse was the high bidder, at $1,750. The following May, the same court ruled that Barbour owed Basse more than $3,500. The court acknowledged Cornelia's interest in the property but put her claim third, behind Hewitt and Basse. When no payment was made, another auction was ordered for 19 May 1870. Again, the high bidder was Basse, who bought the property for $800. Cornelia would have to move, but Basse did not press her to do it quickly.[45]

As this financial meltdown began, Barbour again looked to politics as a means of improving his prospects. Perhaps Frederick Douglass, who gave his best-known lecture, "Self-Made Men," in Alton in March 1868, energized him to try to rise above his difficulties. Late in the year, a local convention of "colored" people met in Alton to elect delegates to a state convention scheduled for January 1869 in Springfield. Participants in the county convention were elected at the precinct level, and Barbour's neighbors sent him to represent them at the meeting. The committee on nominations brought six names to the floor for three slots at the state convention: Isaac Kelly, Daniel Wilkerson, Reverend J. W. Malone, Hezekiah Ellsworth, George W. Anderson, and Barbour. Instead of voting by secret ballot, the convention chose to have delegates come forward when their name was called. The delegates then instructed the secretary to add their name to one of six lists. As might be expected, the electioneering took place with "considerable zeal" and energy, even as the delegates were voting. In such an open procedure, the outcome was clear before the final votes were cast, and those who lost knew it before they were officially told. The convention chose Reverend Malone, Anderson, and Wilkerson. Two of the most visible black men in Alton, Kelly and Barbour, were defeated. Barbour refused take no for an answer and simply showed up at the Springfield meeting, demanding to be seated.[46]

The Springfield convention, after some hesitation, allowed Barbour to participate, but clearly events were not going his way. He had spent the entire year trying to find a way to preserve his solvency and status. He made speeches at public events and revisited politics, but neither provided the lifeline he needed. His financial difficulties were becoming acute. The novelty quickly wore off of his restaurant-style service on the *Belle of Alton*, and the railroad line on which his restaurant and hotel sat, fed its riders on the cars. He opened another restaurant called, significantly, Delmonico, but it also failed. And his huge debt to Basse was due in less than a year. A proud man—one of his main concerns in his first letter to Governor Yates had been to avoid public humiliation—Barbour once again began looking to make a change. By mid-1869, he was investigating business opportunities in Arkansas.[47]

The evidence suggests that, although Barbour attained some stature in the white community during his years in Alton, he may have not been as esteemed by the black community. He was not a churchgoer, although Frances was on the membership list of the Union Baptist Church in 1864 and his daughters were later active in the Campbell African Methodist Episcopal Church. When the black Masons organized in Alton in May 1867, the most prominent men in the city were listed as members, but Barbour was not among them. Having served and sought the approbation of the white community, Barbour may have made his ties to black Alton tenuous. He had friends, of course. Murray Knight, a former slave and now a restaurant owner in nearby Edwardsville, named one of his sons Conway Barbour Knight. In any case, the dual disappointment of being thwarted in both the political and business realms turned Barbour toward a new path.[48]

He left Alton for Lewisville, Arkansas, leaving his family behind. Letters between Barbour and Arkansas governor Powell Clayton's personal secretary demonstrate that he was living in the state and actively courting a political position as of June 1870. In that year, as in 1860, census takers found him in two different places, Alton and Lewisville.

Barbour's experience as a businessman in Alton in the 1860s suggests that, although African Americans could and did achieve some level of success, it may have become more difficult after the Civil War, in part because of a general economic contraction at the end of the conflict. Barbour earned his reputation at the Mercantile during the war (1863–65). That establishment was full, patronized and appreciated by whites like the editor Dowdall. Buoyed by his success, Barbour sought to go bigger, despite the postwar economic downturn. When the new train depot was completed in 1867, Barbour seized the opportunity to establish a luxurious hotel and restaurant on its premises, confident that the location would ensure success. He was wrong. The economy remained depressed, and the railroad itself undermined him by adding dining cars in 1868. The Union Hotel, instead of bringing Barbour the financial solvency and public celebrity he desired, took him deeply, irreparably into debt. Few people stayed there, even though other hotels in town had boarders sufficient to sustain them.

Barbour's race probably contributed to the failure of the Union. Alton was a racist city in a state that affirmed its prejudices during a war for freedom. His success at the Mercantile and the short-lived Fifth Avenue Hall may have given him the idea that the rules, written and unwritten, did not apply to him. By establishing himself in the railroad depot, Barbour greatly increased his visibility and may have stepped outside the acceptable boundaries for African Americans in Alton. If so, his activities in the black community in 1868 may have actually exacerbated his problems. What is clear is that his fortunes fell each time he reached higher. Barbour could operate "a good house." Perhaps, however, he was not supposed to operate *too good* a house.

At the end of the decade, Barbour, as he had in Louisville and Cleveland, saw possibilities elsewhere. In July 1869, he visited Arkansas, ostensibly to reconnoiter the state for some unnamed families seeking to relocate. "Well pleased" with what he saw, Barbour tried to set himself up as a kind of middleman, promising free or cheap land to immigrants, and laborers to the locals. He opened a Labor Exchange Office near the capitol building in Little Rock in December 1869 and, as he had done in Alton, advertised his business heavily in the local paper. The Labor Exchange could furnish "laborers, cooks, and house servants" to all who desired them, he said, as well as town lots and acreage to be sold low on easy terms. Despite support from the state's commissioner on immigration, the exchange folded in the first half of 1870. Its proximity to the statehouse, however, put Barbour in contact with the most powerful men in government, Republicans eager to enlist black allies. Perhaps all was not lost.[49]

James Barbour, Virginia governor, U.S. senator, and secretary of war, was part of the family that gave Conway Barbour his surname. Conway was said to be "a favorite servant" of the governor. 1873 OIL PAINTING BY HENRY ULKE. WIKIMEDIA COMMONS.

William H. Gibson, Barbour's friend in Louisville, was a musician, a teacher, and an activist. His 1897 memoir described the city's African American community in the years before the Civil War. FROM GIBSON'S MEMOIR. WIKIMEDIA COMMONS.

Martin Robison Delany organized the National Emigration Convention of Colored People in Cleveland in 1854. Barbour represented Kentucky at the meeting. UNDATED PHOTO. WIKIMEDIA COMMONS.

Barbour met John Mercer Langston at the emigration convention. In 1866 Conway cosponsored Langston's visit to Alton to speak alongside James Milton Turner. LANGSTON AT HOWARD UNIVERSITY. WIKIMEDIA COMMONS.

Barbour advertised liberally in the *Alton Telegraph* in the 1860s. *ALTON TELEGRAPH* AT NEWSPAPERS.COM.

Henry Basse, a German immigrant, owned a flour mill, restaurants, and a lot of property. He financed Barbour's businesses in Alton.
PHOTO COURTESY OF RON THOMASSIN.

Isaac Kelly was the most prominent black businessman in Alton, owning a barbershop and a bathhouse. Unlike Barbour, Kelly was active in the church and freemasonry.
PHOTO COURTESY OF ALTON MUSEUM OF HISTORY AND ART.

Murray Knight was Barbour's friend in Alton. Like Barbour, the former slave was a caterer and a restaurant owner. PHOTO COURTESY OF PAM BROUSSARD-PATELIS.

Murray Knight named one of his sons after Barbour. Conway Barbour Knight was a chef in Alton for more than forty years. PHOTO COURTESY OF GRETCHEN GRAVES.

Arkansas governor Powell Clayton supported Barbour's election to the state legislature in 1871. Barbour was loyal to the governor and was rewarded for that loyalty. PHOTO TAKEN IN THE 1870S. WIKIMEDIA COMMONS.

James W. Mason was the son of Arkansas's largest antebellum slave owner. He and Barbour were political rivals in Chicot County. PHOTO COURTESY OF JOHN E. BUSH IV.

Conway might be buried in the Barbour family plot in Upper Alton Cemetery, but the cemetery's records do not include him. PHOTO BY SAMUEL D. HARRISON.

Frances outlived Conway by almost forty years. Her headstone memorializes him as much as her. PHOTO BY SAMUEL D. HARRISON.

MRS. CURRY, THE PLAINTIFF.

This drawing of Barbour's daughter Josephine appeared on the front page of the *Chicago Tribune*. It is one of the few depictions of Barbour's children. *CHICAGO TRIBUNE* AT NEWSPAPERS.COM.

Named after Conway's son Thomas, grandson Thomas Conway Rankin was the only member of the family to produce descendants. PHOTO COURTESY OF THE RANKIN FAMILY.

FOUR

Little Rock

BARBOUR'S HARD LANDING in Alton did not diminish his belief that success could be found if one only looked in the right place. At the turn of the decade, then, he was again in motion. When he had left Louisville in the mid-1850s, the South was an oppressive and dangerous place for a man of color. Now, some fifteen years later, the region was in flux and offered political opportunities for blacks that were unimaginable before the Civil War. Millions of freedmen, supplemented by northern blacks like Barbour who went south during Reconstruction, meant voting strength that produced two U.S. senators, sixteen U.S. congressmen, more than six hundred state legislators, and some fourteen hundred other state and local officials after 1867. These black Republicans and a few black Democrats were central to the "unfinished revolution" in the South during these years.[1]

Seizing on these new opportunities, Barbour was elected to the Arkansas legislature after only around a year in the state. He accomplished this by allying with Governor Powell Clayton, leader of the dominant faction in Arkansas's Republican Party, a party rent by internal dissension and under assault by Democrats. Barbour's short term in the Arkansas General Assembly was characterized by intense political warfare as Clayton's enemies tried to remove him from office and thwart his political agenda. Barbour emerged as one of the governor's most strident supporters. In Little Rock, Barbour learned the means and methods of political survival. He entered the legislative session with minimal political experience and left it believing himself a seasoned operative. Barbour achieved the public visibility and success that had slipped away from him in the North when he became one of only a small number of black state legislators in Reconstruction Arkansas.

Arkansas's demography limited the number of African Americans elected to state offices during Reconstruction. In 1870, blacks made up only about 23 percent of the population, and only forty-six African Americans served at the state level before Arkansas was redeemed in 1874. This is consistent with a pattern throughout the South. In Virginia, for example, where whites outnumbered blacks by two to one, relatively few blacks (eighty-five) held state offices during the period. By contrast, South Carolina, where blacks outnumbered whites, was the only state in which blacks held a majority of the seats in the House of Representatives and half of those in the Senate between 1872 and 1876. In no state, however, did blacks control the government, an interpretation popularized by William Dunning and his students in the early twentieth century. The Dunning school ridiculed southern black political participation as evidence of northern vindictiveness. Northern radicals, according to the Dunning-school version of Reconstruction, imposed unprepared black leaders on a defeated, contrite southern white population, and chaos ensued.[2]

Black historians such as A. A. Taylor and W. E. B. DuBois challenged the view that the black politicians were ignorant and unworthy of their elected positions. Instead, Taylor and DuBois saw the men as deserving of praise for their efforts to improve the lives of southern blacks. This revisionist interpretation was adopted with vigor in the 1960s, as monographs appeared that seemed to replace the old stereotype with a new one of black political brilliance and unvarnished heroism. When other historians looked critically at the black legislators, they found a more complicated and interesting story that varied from state to state and undermined both stereotypes. North Carolina's legislative contingent was described in one study covering 1868 to 1872 as not always voting as a unit and failing in most of its attempts to enact reform. Another study of the same group between 1868 and 1870 found a high level of group cohesion, more influence, and a punitive attitude toward former rebels. Arkansas's black delegates to the state's 1868 constitutional convention were literate property holders who almost always functioned as a unit. Unlike the North Carolinians, they did not seem interested in restricting the voting rights of Confederates and were less confrontational toward whites than those portrayed elsewhere. One study of a group of black politicians in Tennessee found ambitious, aggressive, and violent men interested in the educational rights of the freedmen but more often interested in their own elevation.[3]

Other historians looked within the ranks of black politicians and found racial and social divisions at odds with viewing the black community as a "classless lump." David Rankin said elite blacks in New Orleans differed greatly in racial makeup as well as social and economic status from those they sought to lead. A study of South Carolina's black political leadership charged them with being too bourgeois in outlook to focus on the needs of the state's blacks. Georgia's African American politicians, by contrast, many of them ministers in the antebellum, were said to lack the bourgeois skills necessary to defend themselves because of a tendency to accommodate white authority in the Democratic Party. The importance of these socioeconomic cleavages can be overstated, and neither New Orleans nor South Carolina was typical of southern black demography. But even a leading skeptic of this line of inquiry noted that the free-labor ideology of many black leaders separated them in meaningful ways from other southern freedmen.[4]

More recent scholarship on Reconstruction politics has taken a pragmatic approach that critically examines Republican policies and leadership and moderates revisionists' stress on racism as the predominant driver of events. The problem with this historiographical trajectory, according to historian Michael W. Fitzgerald, is that "it deemphasizes African American political behavior when their views most counted." Perhaps wary of criticizing black politicians, historians sometimes "sanitize black politics through omission" or write celebratory depictions of flawed men. Other studies of black politicians and their Reconstruction activities have recognized their "moral lapses," desire for patronage, extreme partisanship, and infighting. As political actors, African Americans could be just as sincere and as greedy, as high-minded and as venal, as their white counterparts. They were human beings, not caricatures.[5]

Although there were corrupt individuals among these officeholders, most were committed to elevating the freed people of the South. Northern-born blacks, often ministers or veterans or both, went south to do good both during and after the war. They went at the behest of the American Missionary Association, the Freedmen's Bureau, or on their own. Some of their names—Tunis Campbell, T. Morris Chester, Robert Elliot, for example—are familiar, but most are not. Ohio-born William B. Barrett, a Civil War veteran, went to New Orleans to fight for black suffrage. New York's Benjamin Boseman, a physician, fought for the care of the mentally ill and orphans in South Carolina. Fellow New Yorker Isaiah Lyons, who served in the Virginia state senate, was fine with separate black schools as long as they employed black teachers. Pennsylvania's James W. Hood, a delegate to North Carolina's 1868 constitutional convention, agreed with Lyons on the importance of having black teachers for black children, but he opposed codifying segregation in the state's "organic law." Having served their brethren as best they could, many of these men returned to the North after redemption of the southern states.[6]

More commonly, Reconstruction officeholders were southern-born men. Some had never left the South, while others left or escaped and then returned during or after the war to assist the freedmen. Thomas Bayne, born a slave in North Carolina, was sold several times before ending up in Norfolk, Virginia, whence he escaped into the North. A dentist and preacher, Bayne returned to Norfolk at the end of the war and served in Virginia's constitutional convention. Virginia slave Daniel Norton escaped to New York, where he trained to be a doctor. He returned to Virginia in 1864 and served in the state senate. His two brothers, Frederick and Robert, were also Reconstruction officeholders. The Hodges, a well-off free family of Virginia, moved to New York in the 1830s after a son was accused of forging free papers for slaves. Four Hodges sons, including the accused, returned to Virginia after the Civil War and served in office. Theophile Allain of Louisiana was a slave but treated as free by his planter father. Educated privately and, after the war, in New Jersey, Allain returned home in 1869 to become a planter himself and serve in the state legislature.[7]

Northern or southern, freeborn or enslaved, educated or illiterate, many officeholders endured death threats, mobs, and other attacks while trying to serve their neighbors. At least thirty-five black politicians were murdered during the period. The dangers were real, and yet the men persevered. Some certainly shared the sentiments of Benjamin Randolph. In 1865, the freeborn, educated minister asked the Freedmen's Bureau for an assignment. "I don't ask position or money," he wrote. "But I ask a place where I can be most useful to my race."[8]

Conway Barbour, seeking political opportunities in Arkansas in 1870, was genuinely interested in the reform agenda of southern Republicans but also thought of politics as an avenue toward economic solvency and public recognition. He ingratiated himself with the Clayton administration in Little Rock and, at its behest, traveled to Lewisville in the southwestern corner of the state, a place so dangerous for freedmen that Governor Clayton had only recently lifted martial law. From this remote and troubled region, Barbour launched his new career as one of what Eric Foner called "freedom's lawmakers." An unknown black man in a strange place, Barbour could only have done so with Clayton's assistance. The two men seem to have struck a bargain: Clayton and his supporters would get Barbour elected, and Barbour would back the governor as he implemented his policies and fought off his political adversaries. It was a profitable arrangement for both men.

If reconstructing Arkansas seemed promising for Barbour, the state's other residents, native and otherwise, were still battling over the implications of the Civil War. Men who had profited from antebellum social, economic, and political structures were eager to resuscitate their moribund society to the degree that they could. The freedmen and many whites, including newcomers to the state, were just as intent on creating a new Arkansas fashioned after an idealized North, promising racial inclusion and a diversified economy. These two visions clashed as some Arkansans looked to the future and others tried to hold on to the past.

Prosperity blessed the Arkansas economy in the years before the war, although the good times were based on a precarious platform of cotton prices and foreign credit. Between 1850 and 1860, economic expansion meant more acreage in cotton and more slaves to tend it. The crop was the most important contributor to the state's economic well-being by the end of the decade. In 1860, Arkansas produced more than 360,000 bales of ginned cotton worth an estimated $16 million; the approximately 111,000 slaves who cultivated the crop were valued at $100 million. Plantation agriculture was the basis for prosperity in the southern portion of the state, even as small farming remained the norm in the mountainous north.[9]

Inadequate transportation, however, put even the most prosperous planters at the mercy of outside forces. Those Arkansans who lived near rivers did better economically, but even they were vulnerable to New Orleans merchants who charged what they wished for supplies and the transport and sale of annual output. Although many cotton planters were rich and lived well, they relied on forces beyond their control. Railroads might have reduced this dependence, but lack of capital and an unwillingness to invest in anything other than acreage and slaves meant that only sixty-six miles of track existed in Arkansas in 1861. Arkansas's prosperity, then, was fragile, and the coming of the Civil War meant the end of good times.[10]

Arkansans resisted secession when the Deep South abandoned the Union in the months after Lincoln's election, but sentiment shifted dramatically after Sumter and the president's call for troops in early 1861. The administration's affront to southern sovereignty pushed Arkansas into the Confederacy, an allegiance that proved disastrous for the state. The wealth accumulated in the 1850s dissipated as the raising and outfitting of troops used up what little cash was available, and creditors refused to extend funding on which the economy depended. Planters sought to "cotton" themselves out of financial trouble and refused to grow food even as shortages produced widespread hunger among Confederates soldiers, Union troops who were deployed in the area, and noncombatants. Deprivation, ruthless enforcement of conscription, and the seizure of private property including slaves created pessimism among the law abiding and anarchy among the less so. In the contest for scarce resources, no one, regardless of their politics, was safe. Confederates stole, Union men stole, and neighbor stole from neighbor in a battle for survival. The rule of law suffered outside the Union stronghold of Little Rock as the war destroyed the land, crippled the economy, and evaporated $100 million in personal property in the form of slaves who fled from the plantations. The slaves' perceived betrayal produced a virulent racism that became the centerpiece of postwar conservatism.[11]

Early efforts at Reconstruction in Arkansas demonstrated that many of its residents did not equate military defeat with social revolution. Their refusal to accept the racial implications of the war put the state at odds with the Republican-controlled federal Congress. In 1864, after meeting the requirements of Lincoln's 10 percent plan, Unionists from less than half the state's counties met to formulate a new constitution. The document forbade slavery and repudiated secession, but it did not give freedmen the vote. The small number of qualified voters ratified the constitution and elected a new governor, Isaac Murphy, and a state legislature in March. That legislature selected two new U.S. senators, but the Congress refused to seat them.[12]

By 1865, as Conway Barbour sold the Mercantile Restaurant and made plans for the Fifth Avenue Hall in Alton, Confederates regained control of some local offices in Arkansas and used them to punish Unionists. Widespread violence continued in late 1865 and into 1866. The Murphy government, unable to quell the disturbances, faced increasing opposition as the congressional elections approached in late 1865. Turnout was low for the election, so Congress again refused to seat the winners. Conservatives were encouraged by their relatively strong showing and also by a state supreme court ruling that declared disfranchisement of former Confederates unconstitutional.[13]

In the state elections in 1866, members of the newly organized Conservative Party argued that Arkansans must save themselves from the dangers of black suffrage and seek tax relief. It was a winning platform for reenfranchised Confederates, and the Conservatives swept the election, placing the old economic elite back in charge in Little Rock. Overriding Governor Murphy's vetoes, the Conservatives legislated their two major goals, tax reduction and labor laws benefiting landlords. As historian Carl Moneyhon argued, the Conservative Sixteenth General Assembly was "not completely reactionary" and, for example, provided funds for new railroads. Nonetheless, just as the Republican Congress feared, lenient Reconstruction policies facilitated a return to power of men who had taken Arkansas out of the Union.[14]

This Conservative resurgence was thwarted when Congress asserted its control over Reconstruction policy in 1867. As Barbour considered giving up Fifth Avenue Hall in favor of better facilities in the Union Depot, the First Reconstruction Act placed Arkansas in the Fourth Military District under the command of General Edward O. C. Ord. Legislation passed by the Sixteenth General Assembly was placed in abeyance as Ord began the process for elections in November 1867 to decide on a new constitutional convention. Conservatives were almost frantic in the face of these reversals, accompanied as they were by crop failures in both 1866 and 1867. Unionists, on the other hand, were so pleased that they organized as Republicans, a moniker previously eschewed. Arkansas's first Republican Party convention met in April 1867, a group comprising native Arkansans loyal to the Union during the war, carpetbaggers, and blacks.[15]

The Republican program, the "New Era," called for internal improvements, free education, and new taxes, all of which threatened propertied Conservatives who feared that economic diversification and education would distract black laborers from work in the fields. The prospect of black political participation was anathema to former Confederates, many of whom could not vote because of provisions in the Reconstruction Act. In November, qualified electors approved the convention and sent a majority of Republicans to Little Rock to write a new constitution. As Conservatives anticipated, the document gave the vote to all adult males except those who had sworn to uphold the U.S. Constitution and then violated that oath by participating in or supporting the rebellion. The franchise restrictions were harsher than those found in other southern state constitutions, but in its mixture of idealism and partisanship, the new Arkansas Constitution was not as peculiar as Conservatives charged. With its voting restrictions, expansion of executive power, and elaborate amendment procedures, the constitution solidified Republican control of the political machinery in the state.[16]

Arkansas's Republican Party, however, consisted of two hostile factions, native-born Arkansans and northerners who had come to the state during the war or thereafter and stayed. Native men resented the presence and political aspirations of the outsiders. This tension produced a negotiated split ticket for the state elections in March 1868. The Republican gubernatorial candidate was Powell Clayton, a former Union officer with the Fifth Kansas Cavalry who had bought a plantation near Pine Bluff during the war. The lieutenant governor nominee was James Johnson, a native Unionist. The ticket won, and after ratifying the Fourteenth Amendment, the new General Assembly petitioned for Arkansas's readmittance to the Union. Overriding President Johnson's veto, the U.S. Congress approved Arkansas's reentry, and Clayton took the oath as governor in July 1868.[17]

Now firmly in control of state government, the Republicans created a public school system and established a state university; provided for internal improvements, including new levees; and raised taxes. The program quickly administered "an economic pinch on the landed interests of the state." Conservatives, now calling themselves Democrats again, hoped to undo all this after the election later in the year when Arkansans were to select a president and some state officials. A leading Democrat urged disfranchised conservative men to perjure themselves if necessary in order to register and vote.[18]

An outbreak of Klan violence against Republicans, especially blacks, alarmed Clayton sufficiently that he began organizing the state militia in August. To avoid giving the Democrats political ammunition, Clayton waited until the election was over before declaring martial law in ten counties. The use of troops was controversial even among Republicans, and Clayton's militia had little of the materiel necessary for its support, prompting confiscation and impressments of scarce food and livestock that would not be forgotten. Martial law greatly reduced the violence, however, usually because local residents, devastated by the impressments, promised an end to Klan activities in return for removal of troops.[19]

Democratic strength in the election validated Clayton's caution; Republicans won in all three of the state's congressional districts but only narrowly in two of the three contests. Republican political fortunes were further diminished as the economic cost of New Era policies registered with the electorate. State expenditures exploded as did state debt. To offset shortfalls, the Republicans raised taxes and reassessed real estate to its market value, a burden on landowners. Democrats, standard-bearers of the propertied class, decried the moves, and native Republicans, with

Clayton's lieutenant governor at the lead, joined the dissent. Because of disfranchisement, martial law, and taxes, the Clayton administration found itself vulnerable to attacks from within and without.[20]

In 1869, as Barbour's Union Hotel went bankrupt, Arkansas's moderate Democrats and disaffected Republicans joined forces under Johnson to form the Liberal Republican Party in preparation for the 1870 state elections. Charging the Clayton government with profligate spending and corruption, the Liberal Republicans of Arkansas joined a larger movement of unhappy Republicans abandoning Clayton. Conservative Democrats, keen to their political restrictions, viewed the Republican split with interest. What to do? Convinced that a separate slate of their own would only reunify fractured and vulnerable Republicanism, Democrats decided to fuse with Liberal Republicans in order to seize power from Clayton Republicans in the elections in late 1870.

The governor conflated loyalty to the Union, the Republican Party, and Powell Clayton into one indivisible package. He therefore viewed the challenge to his power and program as evidence of persistent treason. As he had protected the tenets of the New Era militarily with martial law, he now prepared to use his command of the state's electoral machinery to defend himself and his policies. And so, as the new decade began, Clayton, beleaguered Republican governor of Arkansas, needed political allies. Barbour, frustrated businessman and political aspirant, needed a new beginning. The two joined forces in the tumultuous last phases of Arkansas's Reconstruction history.[21]

In April 1870, shortly after the closure of Barbour's Labor Exchange, James Barton, Clayton's personal secretary, wrote to Volney V. Smith in Lewisville, Arkansas, seeking, on behalf of the governor, a place for an active, intelligent young man. Smith was the Lafayette County clerk and a former Freedman's Bureau representative. According to Barton, Clayton wanted the applicant to aid Smith as he sought to "control the political element of the county." The man was competent, "perfectly honest, temperate, trusting." Conway Barbour was Barton's man.[22]

Smith was mustered out of the Union Army in 1867 and thereafter assigned to duty in Lewisville, "pending the reconstruction" of Arkansas. He was elected clerk of Lafayette County, published the *Red River Post* with editor James Torrans, and served as postmaster. Even so, he complained to his mother, "I do not like the people here." The Arkansans had "very little use for an [*sic*] Northern man," he said, and so "we can only govern them through fear," a statement that helps explain Clayton's growing political opposition. Smith wrote that his salary was ample, but he earned every penny dealing with "rebels on one side and Negroes on the other." Yet, Smith said he stood "high in the estimation of the Officers of the State," men who now sought his assistance in placing Barbour.[23]

While Barton's description of the hotelier was too complimentary— Barbour was not young and perhaps, in his financial distress, not perfectly honest—an arrangement was concluded. Some weeks later, in early June, Barton wrote to Barbour, by then residing in Lewisville. Barton had sent Barbour $75, but the former steward sought additional funds by submitting Western Transit Insurance forms to the governor's mansion. Barton told Barbour that the governor refused to issue him money through the insurance company and would "pay you out of his own pocket." Short of funds, Barbour sought financial support from his benefactors in Little Rock and tried to launder the transaction through Western Transit. Clayton's refusal to acquiesce to the proposed fraud demonstrated a personal honesty not often credited by his critics. Barbour's behavior was not so exemplary.[24]

Apparently as a part of his erstwhile Labor Exchange, Barbour involved himself in the abduction of a young African American boy. In June, Barton asked Smith to look into the whereabouts of twelve-year-old Albert Coleman, who had been "carried away." The boy was reported to be in Rondo, near Lewisville, living with "Mr. Glass." The boy's father, Charles Coleman of Danville, Virginia, was searching for him. In fact, Albert was living in the home of a black woman, Ann Lewis, although J. B. Glass, a wealthy white farmer in Rondo, may have been his employer. Albert was one of three young men, all with different last names, listed as "farm laborers" in the Lewis household. Barbour's involvement is suggested in Barton's letter of 8 August to Conway: "The boy should be sent on to his Father at once—He is looking for him very anxiously."[25]

Barbour's brief descent into fraud and kidnapping reveal his willingness to do what he thought necessary to survive. The 1870 federal census of Lewisville listed Barbour as living in the home of Hattie Butler, an illiterate African American blacksmith. Butler was married; he and his wife had one child and owned no property. Barbour's occupation was reported as life insurance agent, a misinterpretation of his association with Western Transit Insurance. The difference between his real circumstances in Lewisville, broke and living with strangers, and his apparent circumstances in Alton, a cook with $3,500 in real and personal property, suggests the depth of his financial problems. Yet his prospects for rebound were hopeful. In late June, Barton informed Barbour that the governor would visit him in Lafayette County on or about 10 July, when they could "confer . . . at length." Buoyed by this meeting, Barbour decided to run for the state legislature.[26]

Clayton sought alliances with blacks who could help him politically regardless of their nativity or familiarity with Arkansas and its politics. Relatively few native black Arkansans participated in state politics during Reconstruction; most, like Barbour, came from elsewhere in search of opportunity, to lead the freedmen, and to seek wealth and power. On the eve of the Civil War, Arkansas had fewer free blacks than any other slave state, around seven hundred, although they were subject to legal restrictions commonly applied to free African Americans throughout the South. Free blacks paid taxes and owned property in antebellum Arkansas, but they could not vote, testify against whites in court in some cases, or travel freely without written permits. In the wake of the Dred Scott decision, the Arkansas legislature passed and Elias Conway, then governor, signed a long-debated expulsion law that required free blacks to leave the state by 1 January 1860 or else be sold into slavery for a year. The state's free blacks fled in fear such that only about 144 free people of color remained in the state when the Civil War commenced. The total number of free blacks in Arkansas both before and after the exodus was small, but the expulsion law significantly diminished black free yeomanry and intellectual capital.[27]

Arkansas's former slaves were overwhelmingly rural and uneducated. In 1860, a small percentage of the state's slaves, roughly 3 percent, lived in towns. The other 97 percent lived in the countryside, and almost half of those were on plantations in holdings of twenty-five or more. While generalizations about the skill sets of slaves are usually unhelpful—urban slaves could be unskilled laborers and rural slaves were often trained craftsmen—the vast majority of Arkansas slaves cultivated cotton to the exclusion of other endeavors. Educating slaves was legal but uncommon. Still, many of Arkansas's former slaves brought determination and political savvy into the postwar era, and accompanied by some freeborn men, they fought for rights denied them in the antebellum years.[28]

Some months after the war ended, in November 1865, Arkansas's African American citizens convened in Little Rock to demand education, equality before the law, and land. Led by James T. White, a freeborn Baptist minister from Indiana, the delegates included William H. Grey, who would later be the first African American to address a national political convention (the Republican National Convention of 1872), and a number of former slaves from Arkansas and elsewhere. These men, like their counterparts in Louisville, Cleveland, and Alton, sought the tangible benefits of citizenship promised by the Union victory.[29]

The task was not to be easily accomplished, particularly as conservatives reasserted themselves during presidential Reconstruction. A year after the Little Rock convention, a Freemen's Bureau official reported to the home office that outrages, assaults, and murders of freedmen were being "continually reported from nearly all sections" and that fifty-two murders of freed people by white men had been reported to his office in the previous few months. The violence was particularly serious in the southeastern and southwestern corners of the state. Freedmen who reported mistreatment were "missed and never heard of afterwards," and the actual number of murders was probably much higher than the bureau officially reported.[30]

Although Governor Clayton suppressed the violence with an unpopular declaration of martial law in the most troubled areas, the move, coupled with his New Era program of taxes and internal improvements, helped crystallized his opposition. And while he needed black allies like the newcomer from Alton, Clayton preferred men he could control.

The quick rise and fall of the state's first black newspaper demonstrated that Clayton's support for African Americans correlated directly with their acceptance of his political positions. In 1869, a group of African Americans in Little Rock began organizing the creation of a black newspaper, the *Arkansas Freeman*. Reverend Tabbs Gross became proprietor and editor. Gross, formerly a slave in Kentucky, purchased himself with funds earned from preaching to northern abolitionists. After a speaking tour in Europe, he settled in Cincinnati, where he chaired a "Committee to get Homes for Refugees." He came to Arkansas in 1867 to help in its reconstruction.[31]

The *Freeman* initially received support from both major Little Rock papers, the Democratic *Daily Arkansas Gazette* and the *Little Rock Republican*, edited and owned by Barton. The *Gazette* editors thought the new paper might strengthen black leadership and thereby weaken the hold of "radicals" over the state's African Americans. Gross's paper inspired such hope when it advocated equality for all, specifically, the enfranchisement of thousands of white Arkansans whose privilege had been revoked. Gross believed that blacks had to deal liberally with the Democrats or face retaliation once the party regained control of the state, which he believed was inevitable. He favored amnesty and universal suffrage. The black editor also chided Republicans for failing to support black candidates for office, a mistake Clayton was in the process of correcting. Unhappy with the criticism, Barton's *Republican* not only withdrew its support from the *Freeman* but also sought to destroy the paper by attacking Gross's character. By the summer of 1870, the *Freeman* was out of business.[32]

As Barbour was preparing to run for the state legislature, his backers were quashing an independent black voice in Arkansas politics. New to the state and eager to play a role in Reconstruction, Barbour probably missed the implications of Gross's problems with the Republicans. Barbour needed and continued to receive the governor's support. In August 1870, Barton wrote the former businessman, asking, "Did you receive the money? . . . G[overnor] has been away and has not been able to make any arrangements but will do so."[33]

Barbour quickly adapted to his role as candidate and Republican spokesman, and he was speaking at political rallies by late summer. He spoke on behalf of the Republican candidate in Arkansas's Second Congressional District, Oliver P. Snyder, at a state convention on 4 August, in Camden. As Barbour launched his own bid for the state legislature, he solicited help from his son Joseph, who electioneered for his father at the offices of the *Republican* in October. Joseph told the editors that "his father will be elected to the Legislature from Lafayette District, as well as the whole Republican ticket. Mr. [Conway] Barber [*sic*]," the paper continued, "is a tried Republican and will make a good representative."[34]

Using appointive powers granted by the new constitution, Republicans swept the elections in Lafayette County in November 1870. Barbour received 987 votes in his bid for the Arkansas House, only a few shy of U.S. congressman-elect Snyder's 994. Republican-appointed county registrars determined who could and could not vote, and since those registrars were often themselves candidates for office, skeptics questioned the fairness of their electoral conduct. The registrar in Lafayette County in 1870 was Torrans, Smith's partner at the *Red River Post* and a Republican candidate for the state senate who won with the same vote total as Snyder. The Republicans decided who could vote, and the Republicans won the elections. Without angry opponents seething for vengeance, it might have been political perfection. Unfortunately for Clayton and his supporters like Barbour, enemies of the administration were biding their time. In the meanwhile, Barbour savored his triumph.[35]

Barbour owed his victory to his friends in Lewisville and Little Rock and to his son. He rewarded Joseph by arranging for the former book salesman to serve as one of the three pages in the Arkansas House during the coming session. It was a short-term job; the legislature met every other year and for only about three months. But the position was rather prestigious, and Barbour's ability to bestow it demonstrated his newfound clout. In late 1870, father and son left for Little Rock and the Arkansas General Assembly.

Back home in Cleveland, Joseph's mother, Cornelia, continued to list Conway as head of household in the 1870 and 1871 city directories, suggesting either a lingering hope that he would return to her or a stubborn refusal to admit that she was abandoned. Common sense points to the latter scenario. By 1870, Conway had been married to Frances for more than a decade. Their eighth child, Lillie, was born in Alton in January 1871, around the time Conway took his seat in the Arkansas legislature in the state's capital.

The Civil War and its aftermath transformed Little Rock, a southern capital now inhabited not only by black state legislators but also by a number of black city officials. The 1871 city directory, the first ever issued, showed that several blacks held positions of authority in the municipality, a phenomenon inconceivable only a few years earlier. "Colored" men, duly noted as such in the directory, were policemen, aldermen, and jail guards. Thomas Johnson, of the city's Third Ward, was a justice of the peace with $2,500 in real and personal property. City Marshal William A. Rector, possibly related to or owned by a former governor, had $4,000 in real and $1,200 in personal property. The extent of progress, however, should not be overstated. Of 341 black male heads of household in the directory, 215 (63 percent) were occupied as laborers, teamsters, porters, and draymen. Some, like teamster Osborn Hill, accumulated substantial assets. Hill, a forty-two-year-old Georgia native, had real and personal property worth $2,400. Most of these workers, however, owned nothing.[36]

Black and mulatto women were typically seamstresses or washerwomen who also had no property. A couple of black women were associated with hotel- or saloon-keeping families, but the economic prospects for free black women in postbellum Little Rock were similar to those found in antebellum Louisville and Cleveland or pre- and postwar Alton. An 1870 census entry for a "bawdy house" of white women and the number of poor white laborers in the city directory suggests that times were difficult for many.

Some months before the city directory was published, Barbour went to Little Rock to become a member of the Arkansas General Assembly. Just as Clayton saw defense of the New Era as an extension of the Civil War, Barbour fought the war in his own way in Little Rock by defending the governor. Many years earlier, another governor, Illinois' Richard Yates, declined Barbour's offer to provide leadership in the national crisis. Now, fresh from his electoral victory, Barbour had the chance to defend the meaning of the Civil War as embodied by Clayton and to demonstrate his own political skills by proving, belatedly, that Yates was wrong. Barbour approached the task with energy.

During the eighteenth session of the Arkansas legislature, commencing 2 January 1871, Clayton's opponents tried to neutralize him as a force in Little Rock. They first elected him to the U.S. Senate so that Lieutenant Governor Johnson, a native Arkansan and Liberal Republican, would ascend to the governorship and the statehouse. When Clayton refused to relinquish his office to this political enemy, the Arkansas House next impeached him for political and financial malfeasance. The impeachment effort failed, but the indictment and related political warfare dominated the entire session. The tone was set on the first day when an armed force verified the legislators' credentials.[37]

Barbour was one of ten African Americans negotiating their way through the confusion and rancor. Arkansas's 1871 black legislative contingent, like the Republican Party as whole, split into two factions, Clayton men and anti-Clayton men. Unlike Richard Hume's black delegates to the 1868 Arkansas constitutional convention or Elizabeth Balanoff's North Carolinians, the African American state legislators of 1871 did not vote as a bloc and, like their white colleagues, had differing ideas about the correct course of action. The dissension within their ranks supports the more nuanced view of black Reconstruction politicians advanced by modern scholarship.[38]

The African Americans sat with fifty-six native white Arkansans, fourteen whites from outside the state, and assorted white legislators of unknown nativity. Politically, the fusion ticket of Democrats and Liberal Republicans had thirty-eight seats in the General Assembly, four short of control. The Republicans had a better grip on the state senate, where Democrats were six votes short of a majority. The opposition's strength in the legislature and its vehement hatred for Clayton and his New Era meant a session characterized by ruthless political combat. If Barbour sought the rough and tumble of politics, he found it in Little Rock.[39]

The weapon of choice in the 1871 Arkansas legislature was removal from office through promotion, legal challenge, and/or impeachment. The impeachment of President Andrew Johnson in 1868 gave southerners a model for settling political disagreements. Whereas at the national level, Republicans had used the tool against a Democrat, in the South, Democrats impeached Republicans and Republicans impeached each other in what one historian called "impeachment megalomania." In Florida, Republican legislators tried four times to remove Republican governor Harrison Reed, who had appointed Democrats to office. North Carolina governor William W. Holden, a Republican, was successfully removed in 1870 by conservatives who were angry over his use of martial law to put down the Klan. Several years later, Republican Mississippi governor Adelbert Ames resigned rather than defend himself against a thirteen-count indictment that had more to do with Democratic opposition to educating blacks than any real malfeasance. His black lieutenant governor, A. K. Davis, also impeached, resigned first so that the state would not have an African American governor even for a while. Political allies of the targets, usually judges, were also impeached for real or manufactured offenses.[40]

In Arkansas, Clayton's opposition moved cautiously and tried first to remove him with a promotion. A little more than a week into the session, on 10 January 1871, the House voted to send Clayton to the U.S. Senate for a term beginning 4 March. Seventy-one of the House members voted for Clayton, including all but one of the African Americans. This overwhelming show of support, however, masked the true intent of many of the legislators. Conservatives and Liberal Republicans wanted Clayton out of the state so that Johnson could replace him. Clayton knew this and withheld any formal acceptance of the new position.[41]

In the meanwhile, Clayton's Republican allies sought to enhance their voting strength in the House by successfully challenging the electoral legitimacy of a native white Democrat from Lawrence County. Barbour served on a committee that determined the man was illegally elected and should be replaced by his Republican opponent. Even though the Republican received far fewer votes in the election, he was seated and the Democrat removed.[42]

Encouraged, the Republicans tried to impeach the lieutenant governor to remove him from the line of succession. The attempt, which Barbour supported, failed when conservatives passed a bill indefinitely postponing its consideration. Democrats retaliated by challenging the seats of three Republican legislators. Barbour was a member of the committee that reported in support of the men, but the Republicans were sent home.[43]

By early February, the atmosphere in the chamber was poisoned, and the African American contingent was torn between Clayton supporters, like Barbour, and other African Americans who had broken with the Clayton Republicans on key issues. Although differences among the black legislators mirrored cleavages in the entire body, only one, Edward Fulton, took his complaints to the floor of the House.

Fulton, a census taker born in Kentucky, had been a slave of "Uncle" Levi Goben in Livingston County, Missouri. Residing in Quincy, Illinois, in 1866, Fulton told the Freedman's Bank he had been an "intelligence officer" in the army, although no military records have been found to substantiate the claim. Fulton was a black Republican, but he often voted with the conservatives, helping to block Johnson's impeachment and to remove the three Republican legislators. Other Republicans, black and white, did not appreciate this independence and launched a whisper campaign against him.[44]

On 10 February, Fulton told the other legislators that he had heard, in the chamber and on the streets of Little Rock, that he had "sold out to the [D]emocracy," a charge that he said was levied by liars and scoundrels. Fulton said he was his own man, unlike his accusers, who were in fact under "contract . . . [with] a prominent [D]emocrat in this city." He was a Republican looking after the interest of his constituents. The "truth was not in" anyone who said different.[45]

Fulton's comments demonstrated the vulnerability of those blacks who did not unquestionably adhere to the Republican Party and its program, a lesson Tabbs Gross learned a few years earlier when Little Rock Republicans helped destroy his newspaper. Blacks, like Fulton, who allied with Democrats and Liberal Republicans were accused of selling out, but they often actively defended the rights of African Americans. For example, William Hines Furbush, a volatile mulatto politician who helped create an Arkansas county named for Robert E. Lee, cooperated with Democrats after he perceived Republican corruption, even as he fought for civil rights. Challenging discrimination by a Little Rock bar in 1873, Furbush was represented by attorney Mifflin W. Gibbs, a prominent African American who for a time allied with Clayton's Liberal Republican opponents. Gross and Gibbs later became law partners; Furbush and Fulton later launched a newspaper, the *National Democrat*, in 1889. Arkansas's black politicians, then, were neither unanimously wedded to the Republican Party nor of one mind as to the way to obtain full citizenship, concepts that may have eluded Barbour, whose career depended on the Republican governor.[46]

Yet even Barbour grew frustrated with Clayton. By mid-February, more than a month had elapsed since Clayton had been elected to the U.S. Senate, and he had still not formally accepted or declined the position. The House wanted an answer and voted sixty-one to fifteen to send a delegation to Clayton to get one. Ostensibly a push by conservatives to make Clayton declare himself, the motion was also favored by some Clayton allies, including Barbour. Four other African Americans, including Fulton, voted in the affirmative; the remaining five blacks voted against the measure.[47]

Clayton's response revealed little; he said that he intended to do what was best for the state. His detractors read this as "what is best for Powell Clayton," and they responded swiftly. Within three days, anti-Clayton forces produced six articles of impeachment against the governor. The articles charged him with, among other things, conspiring to deprive Johnson of his office, directing election fraud, taking bribes, and general misconduct and malfeasance. The motion called for Clayton's immediate suspension from office. Fulton was among those appointed to manage the impeachment effort. He was also the only African American who voted for the impeachment, which was approved with forty-two yeas, thirty-eight nays, and two not voting.[48]

Many representatives wanted explanations for their vote on the impeachment entered in the legislature's journal, the organ of the Arkansas House, but Barbour was the only African American to put his reasoning on the record. He said, "While I am willing to vote for the impeachment of any person that lives, I will vote against this for these reasons: First. No law. Second. No precedent. Third. No evidence." The statement was dramatic, but it is improbable that Barbour would have voted to impeach the governor in any case. Barbour actively participated in the legislative attempt to remove the lieutenant governor, the primary charge in the indictment. If that effort was found to be illegal, Barbour could be implicated. Further, Barbour owed his elevation in the political world to Clayton. Protecting the governor was a form of self-defense.[49]

Clayton was prepared to defend himself militarily if necessary. He organized a company of supporters "sworn to stand by their chief and defend him and his throne even unto death." The group was known as the "Invincibles." Secretary of State Ozra A. Hadley was captain; Attorney General J. R. Montgomery, first lieutenant; and Conway Barbour, the only African American to remonstrate with the impeachment on the floor of the House, was second lieutenant. Clayton obtained supplies from the arsenal in Little Rock, enough to arm 100 to 150 men, and placed them in the executive office. The Invincibles never went to battle, but the creation of this paramilitary unit demonstrated the level of tension in Little Rock. Barbour's position as third in command shows how closely allied he was with the governor.[50]

Two days after impeaching the governor, the House brought articles of impeachment against his ally John McClure, chief justice of the Arkansas Supreme Court. The House accused McClure, among other things, of conspiring with Clayton to deny Johnson his rightful place as governor because McClure had ruled that Clayton could not be removed before being convicted of the charges against him. The same team of House managers shepherding the Clayton impeachment, including Fulton, was appointed to pursue the indictment against McClure.[51]

The discussion preliminary to voting was particularly heated, with one conservative ominously asking permission to "pair off" with a colleague who opposed both the Clayton and McClure impeachments. Points of order and procedural questions dominated the debate as members challenged other members' challenges. Finally, the House voted in favor of impeaching the chief justice, with forty-four yeas, thirty nays, and eight not voting.[52]

Barbour and five other African American members voted against impeaching McClure. Fulton and two other blacks did not vote; one black legislator voted in favor. Barbour, again, was the only African American to put a comment in the House's *Journal*. He claimed that the impeachment document was invalid and therefore did not exist. Thus, Barbour declared, "I see nothing before the House."[53]

The impeachment of Clayton on 16 February and the McClure indictment two days later marked the nadir of the eighteenth session of the Arkansas House. Impeachment, verbal attacks, and threats of physical assault were all accepted elements of political discourse in Reconstruction Arkansas and elsewhere in the South. Some Arkansas legislators, however, desired a more civil tone. On 17 February, in between the two impeachments, the House appointed a special committee to look at ways of improving the political climate. Barbour was one of the three members appointed to the committee, a testament to his distinctive role in the session. "Considerable excitement and bad feelings exist among members of this House, and the different co-ordinate branches of this state government," a white legislator observed. The discontent and ill will born of disfranchisement, the tax policy, and the hardball politics of tit-for-tat impeachments had paralyzed the House. The committee was directed to report as early as possible "whether or not, there is any probability or possibility to come to more amicable relations with each other." In that spirit, the House impeached McClure the next day. Even so, the worst was about over.[54]

The Clayton impeachment was in trouble from the start, primarily because the governor's Senate allies would not cooperate. On 21 February, a conservative member facetiously asked that a committee be sent to find seventeen senators who had mysteriously disappeared and to propose "some plan for their restoration to the bosom of their many friends." Clayton's supporters in the Senate simply absented themselves from the body, thereby denying the quorum necessary to proceed on the charges against the governor. On 1 March, the House managers presented a report that concluded no impeachment trial could be had in the Senate and asked to be relieved of their duties.[55]

Barbour initially voted against the motion but then asked that his vote be changed. Referring to the managers, he said, "This is a dodge to get rid of their elephant. Their names were brought in with the articles of impeachment; the wish to get out is a dodge to get their articles out. I therefore vote to get rid of them." Some members objected to this unparliamentary language, but the House agreed to include the comment in its journal.[56]

New managers were impaneled but had no more luck with the Senate than had their predecessors. On 4 March, unwilling to do battle any longer, they too asked to be relieved, and the impeachment charges were dropped. Commenting two days later, Barbour called the Clayton impeachment "a self-evident political trick" aimed at putting Johnson in the governor's mansion. "The parties who got up this trick had no political existence, but were digging in the dirt to get a foundation upon which to erect a political temple," he said. Taking hold of the metaphor, Barbour continued, "Exhausted in their means in digging the hole, leaving them no resource but to tumble in, [they] ask the fresh dug dirt to fall in upon them and cover their shame." Other African Americans also went on record in support of the governor, but Fulton, who was absent when the House voted to stop the impeachment attempt, attached his name to a report presented 7 March by the first team of House managers. The report reaffirmed the managers' certainty of Clayton's guilt. The Clayton impeachment abandoned, the House continued to wrangle over its charges against Chief Justice McClure. House managers reduced the scope of the indictment and finally dropped the matter altogether.[57]

Clayton then conducted his final maneuver. His secretary of state resigned—and was possibly bribed to do so—and Clayton offered to appoint his battered and beaten lieutenant governor to the position. Johnson accepted. On 14 March, the House elected Powell Clayton as U.S. senator for a second time, and Ozra A. Hadley, the Clayton ally at the helm of the Invincibles, became governor of Arkansas.[58]

As might be expected, Clayton had less support this time. He received forty-two votes, including a handful cast by conservatives. Barbour, predictably, supported the governor, as did six other African Americans. Fulton and two other black legislators voted for James T. White, who had organized the state's convention for black citizens in Little Rock in 1865. Fulton paid dearly for his vote. He was "shot and dangerously wounded" by a Clayton supporter in the summer of 1871, a reminder that black independence carried penalties in Reconstruction Arkansas.[59]

The session adjourned on 25 March. The final entry in the House's *Journal* was a message from House Speaker Charles Tankersley. After thanking the members for their uniform courtesy toward him, Tankersley turned to the events of the session. "It is unnecessary . . . for me to allude to the political vicissitudes in this House," he said. "I hope that much which has been said will be curtained in oblivion; and it will be a pleasure to me . . . to know that much which has been done will sleep among the things of the past, to be resurrected nevermore." On that note, Tankersley declared the House adjourned sine die.[60]

The antics of the Eighteenth General Assembly were, as historian Thomas DeBlack has said, "pure political farce." Yet, the legislators found time to enact some of the measures Clayton recommended in his message to a joint meeting of the House and Senate at the beginning of the session. Both chambers approved and the governor signed bills providing for more efficient collection of the public school fund, a new law on levee repairs, and regulation of roads and highways. All benefited the New Era's education and business agenda. The House also took steps to make land more readily available, a matter of great importance to the state's freedmen. In addition, as Clayton urged, the legislature approved a constitutional amendment returning the franchise to former Confederates, the first step toward Arkansas's redemption a few years later. Barbour supported the franchise measure, associating himself with another legislator's comment that no one should be deprived of the vote for political reasons.[61]

As a member of the committees on education, public expenditures, and elections, Barbour considered substantive issues affecting Arkansas's

African Americans and all Arkansans even as he defended Clayton from his political foes. Barbour was actively involved in the effort to reform the state penitentiary, which leased inmates to contractors but obligated the state to supply food, clothing, and medical care for the often-abused inmates. His efforts received a favorable review from the sympathetic *Morning Republican.* Calling Barbour a credit to his party and race, "spicy in debate," and able to manage "perplexing questions," the paper held him up as an example of the rapid advancements made by former bondsmen. He was, however, careful not to appear too militant in defense of African Americans. When his name was attached without his knowledge to the call for a convention of colored men in March, he protested, thereby engendering the wrath of some black Arkansans. As one of the few black Reconstruction-era politicians in Arkansas, Barbour was responsible for looking after the interests of the freedmen he represented and of the man whose backing helped him get those freedmen's votes.[62]

Historian Merline Pitre, analyzing black Reconstruction leadership in Texas, identified five different "personalities" among those politicians: the militant, the party loyalist, the opportunist, the accommodationist, and the "climber of sorts." Her depictions of militant Matthew Gaines and accommodationist Robert L. Smith do not evoke Barbour, who was too concerned with acceptance to be a militant and too proud to be an accommodationist. He is better described as an amalgam of her other three categories, because Barbour was a loyalist, an opportunist, and a climber. Like George Ruby, Barbour was unquestionably loyal to the Republican Party, to Clayton, and to his policies. Like Richard Allen, who lost interest in a "black reservation" as the solution for Texas's African Americans when it failed to serve his political ambition, Barbour moved from emigration to patriotism and to service as it suited his needs. Like Norris Wright Cuney, Barbour tried to climb the ladder of success for its own rewards. Pitre, sympathetic to the black Texas legislators, suggests that they were often diverted from their goals by the realities of their vulnerable positions but served creditably in a hostile environment.[63]

In Arkansas, Barbour had an opportunity to fight for the something larger than himself and to make his mark as a man of some consequence to the issues of the day. He was determined to protect his newfound stature to the point of taking up arms, if necessary, as Clayton's highest-ranking black Invincible. In Little Rock, Barbour achieved the public visibility that had eluded him in his previous turns as an emigrationist and businessman. His self-confidence rebounded. Having advertised himself while in

Alton as having three decades of experience on the country's best steam-boats, he claimed during a debate on the penitentiary bill in Little Rock to have the "knowledge of twelve years [*sic*] experience of a good financier," an odd claim given his economic difficulties. If he did not forget them, he at least put out of mind the financial woes that had beset him in Illinois. After his short term in the legislature, Barbour anticipated new oppor-tunities, and Clayton provided them.[64]

Shortly after the legislative session, Clayton's successor appointed Bar-bour tax assessor for Chicot County, Arkansas, in the deep southeastern portion of the state. This would be Barbour's last move. Having honed his political skills in Little Rock, he took those talents into a new arena with even greater challenges.

FIVE

Lake Village, Arkansas

CONWAY BARBOUR CONSIDERED himself a man of influence when he left Little Rock in the late spring of 1871. Having served ably as a defender of then governor, now senator, Powell Clayton during a tumultuous three months in the Arkansas legislature, Barbour obtained the patronage appointment he desired and expected for his exertions. In this last phase of Arkansas Reconstruction, however, Barbour found that opportunities for African Americans were restricted, not only by those who had never accepted black political participation, but also by friends who abandoned them when it became expedient to do so. If Barbour's tenure in Little Rock revealed the possibilities for northern black allies of southern Republicans during Reconstruction, his years in Lake Village were to demonstrate the ongoing importance of localism and resistance to outsiders regardless of race. As Barbour sought to capitalize on the political benefits borne by his race and political connections, he found that neither served him well in southeastern Arkansas. Instead, he encountered a pervasive violence that pitted natives against newcomers, race against race, and Republicans against one another, often with lethal results. In Chicot County, the ability to mobilize a mob was the political credential that mattered.

Chicot County was cotton country. In the years before the Civil War, the county was home to some of the largest, wealthiest plantations in the state. At the outset of the war, almost four of every ten landowners in the county had plantation-sized slaveholdings; in 1860, eight different people in Chicot owned more than one hundred slaves. One of those individuals, Elisha Worthington, owner of the Sunnyside, Redleaf, Meanie, and Eminence plantations, had 543 slaves and twelve thousand acres of land; he was the largest slaveholder in antebellum Arkansas. Worthington, a Kentuckian, migrated to Chicot in the 1830s and purchased a piece of Sunnyside in 1840, the same year he married Mary Chinn. The marriage lasted only a short while because of Worthington's relationship with one of his female slaves. The Kentucky legislature granted Mary Worthington a divorce and restored her maiden name in 1843. Further violating southern social norms, Elisha Worthington raised the two children of his slave mistress as his own and in his household. His son became Barbour's rival as the former House member sought to become the "boss" of Chicot County in the years after his service in Little Rock. Whereas Barbour presumed that his political experience would lead to local prominence, Worthington's son took authority as a birthright.[1]

The Worthington children, James W. and Martha Mason, were privileged by their father's wealth and affection, elite blacks among thousands of slaves. Both attended Oberlin, and James studied at St. Cyr, a military academy in France. By one account, he fought for the French in the Crimean War. When the Civil War came to Chicot County, Worthington took a number of his slaves and headed for Texas, leaving his two children to care for his property, another sign of their elevated stature in the community. After the war, Worthington returned to Chicot County with many of his former slaves and regained control of his plantations after being pardoned by Andrew Johnson in 1866. The land was devastated by warfare and neglect, and Worthington, suffering from health and financial problems, started selling off property. He moved to Redleaf, where daughter Martha cared for him until his death in 1873.[2]

Meanwhile, Worthington's son, James Mason, took up politics. He was a delegate to the Arkansas Constitutional Convention of 1868 and was appointed, but declined to become, U.S. minister resident and consul general to Liberia in 1870. Mason served in the Arkansas Senate while Barbour was in the House in 1871. Considered a man of ability, Mason, along with fellow senator James T. White, was compared favorably to the black legislators in the House. Well born and well connected, Mason might have been a valuable ally to Barbour, his fellow Republican. Unfortunately for Barbour, the two men became enemies instead of friends. Their shared biracial backgrounds meant nothing as the outsider and the local man vied for political dominance in Chicot County.[3]

In the spring of 1871, Governor Ozra A. Hadley appointed Barbour as tax assessor and Mason as county and probate judge, a gubernatorial prerogative under the state constitution. Both appointments were contested, and both Barbour and Mason had to fight for their positions. After they beat their opponents and assumed their offices, they turned on each other. The chaotic Arkansas General Assembly was decorum itself compared with the political atmosphere in Lake Village, where issues of money, race, and power intersected to produce hatreds and retributions fundamentally tied to the issues of the late Civil War.

The demographic and political changes in Chicot County between 1860 and 1870 help explain its volatile atmosphere. Before the war, the county's roughly 1,700 white residents held dominion over a slave population in excess of 7,500. There were no free people of color in the county in the 1860 census. A decade later, after a devastating war, crop failures in 1866 and 1867, and disfranchisement of whites aligned with the Confederacy, about 1,800 whites lived among more than 5,000 freedmen with voting rights. Former slaves were now politically powerful, and that offended many whites suffering from the economic consequences of the war.

Because of its location along the Mississippi River, Chicot County suffered more than other areas of the state during the conflict. The same river that carried antebellum cotton to New Orleans delivered Union troops to the county during the Civil War. The cash value of Chicot County farms fell from $4.4 million in 1860 to less than $1.5 million in 1870, about 66 percent; by contrast, the value of farms in Lafayette County, which Barbour represented in the House, fell over the same period from $2.3 million to $1.2 million, or 49 percent. Chicot County had forty-eight farms of more than five hundred acres in 1860 but only twenty-three such farms in 1870, a decrease of 52 percent. In Lafayette County, the respective numbers were twenty-five and twenty, a drop of 20 percent. Chicot County's antebellum elite were further alienated by Clayton's New Era policies of high taxes and universal education and by constitutional disfranchisement that restricted their ability to resist at the ballot box.[4]

Even so, Chicot County's white residents remained better off economically than its blacks and mulattos, who owned little despite their new political power. In McConnell Township, home to county-seat Lake Village, for example, thirty-four of the township's seventy-four white heads of household owned real property worth more than $350,000 in 1870. Three white heads of household owned roughly two-thirds of that sum, $220,000, on three large plantations. Forty-four white heads of household had personal property valued at around $65,000. By contrast, only two of the township's 311 black heads of household owned property; one with property valued at $5,000, the other with real property worth only $25. The twenty-two mulatto heads of household owned no real estate. About one-third of black heads of household owned personal property (93 of 311) worth a total of $16,000; nine mulattos owned a total of only $1,665.[5]

Despite their continuing economic power, many Chicot County whites could see only what they had lost and blamed their misfortunes on the blacks, who were now enfranchised and holding offices in the county, and on their white allies, many of whom were from the North. Unknown blacks, like Barbour, were particularly objectionable as they had no history in the county and lacked the deference that prewar elites and other whites expected of blacks. Barbour, who knew little of Lafayette County when he had represented it in the legislature, understood little more of Chicot County politics when he was sent there in 1871 as its new tax assessor.

He understood well, though, that land ownership signified independence and status. Before he left Little Rock, he had applied for and received donation acreage in Chicot County from the Arkansas Commissioner of State Lands Office. Donation lands were acres forfeited to the state for nonpayment of taxes. All of Arkansas was originally owned by the federal government, which made land available to settlers at prices so affordable that many simply abandoned it when better opportunities presented themselves. Those lands reverted to the county and, if unsold, to the state.

Beginning in 1840, the Arkansas legislature gave the state auditor, and later the land commissioner, a process by which to return the acreage to people who were supposed to cultivate the land and pay taxes on it. By 1871, the revised law provided that any head of household could claim 160 acres for himself and additional sections for his wife and each minor child.[6]

About a week after the close of the General Assembly, Barbour applied for land on behalf of himself, Frances, and six minor children. Two of the minors were children from his first marriage, to Cornelia, although it is unlikely he had seen them in more than a decade. He also claimed acreage for three of his children by Frances but not for their youngest daughters, Minnie, born in 1869, and Lillie, born in January 1871. The sixth minor was his daughter-in-law Virginia, Thomas's wife.

While other former legislators availed themselves of the donation statutes, none was as aggressive as Barbour in seeking this free land. Edmund Wiley, a white lawyer from Illinois who represented Arkansas County in the 1871 legislative session, claimed acreage for himself and three family members. John Webb, a black House member and justice of the peace in Chicot County, obtained land for himself and two minors. James Mason acquired land for himself and his wife, Marie, possibly because his father's prewar holdings were being sold. Barbour claimed land on behalf of eight people, about 1,100 acres, more than any other politician from southeastern Arkansas. And although the donation laws were intended to facilitate reclamation and development of state lands, Barbour never lived on or cultivated his claim and did not pay the taxes owed on it until he prepared to sell the acreage several years later. Even so, he traveled to Chicot County as a large landowner with a lucrative government job.[7]

Expecting the same welcome he had received in Lewisville and Little Rock, Barbour quickly discovered that neither his résumé nor his race carried weight when he arrived in Lake Village in late April. The Republican legislature had set the salaries for appointed officials in predominately black counties much higher than for those named to positions in majority white areas. These few high-paying positions, including the tax assessor's slot, were coveted, and native Chicotians, black and white, presumed one of their own would receive the appointment. When Barbour went to Lake Village and announced himself as the new assessor, they rebelled. He was told that "the room was better than his company" and that "it would be better for his health if he made himself scarce." He stayed two days and then left, fearful for his safety. Complicating matters was the fact that Barbour was initially unaware that another man, Frank Downs, a Canadian-born lawyer, had also been appointed tax assessor of Chicot County. In the economically crippled county, any outsider claiming a well-paid county post, particularly one responsible for setting local residents' tax burden, was cause for revolt. And now there were two, although there is no record that Downs encountered the same hostile reception that Barbour did.[8]

Mason, a county native and the manor-born son of Elisha Worthington, had his own contestant for the county judge position. Former governor Clayton promised Mason, then a state senator, the judgeship in exchange for support when the Arkansas legislature voted the first time to send Clayton to Washington. Mason's state senate colleagues, however, "passed over" Mason's confirmation and did not consider it, so Clayton ordered that another man, Major Ragland of Jefferson County, receive the appointment. A federal investigation of Clayton's activities determined later that a deal had been made before the second vote on Clayton's senatorial election in the General Assembly and that both Mason and James T. White had been bribed and were, by the way, "very expensive."[9]

When both Mason and Ragland tried to take the bench in Lake Village in May 1871, the county sheriff, Franklin P. Walker, sided with Ragland and threatened to put Mason in jail. As the confrontation played out, Ragland lost his nerve, leaving Mason "master of the field." When the exposed sheriff left town, Mason sent a posse to arrest him for contempt of court. Judge Mason ordered Walker confined, but since no one, oddly, could find the keys to the jail, he was released.[10]

The difficulties in Chicot County should have been unsettling to a stalwart Clayton loyalist like Barbour. Courting support for his Senate bid, Clayton had promised positions to whomever he happened to need at any particular moment, forgetting or ignoring previous promises. He appointed Downs and Mason, and then a couple of days after the legislative session ended, Hadley, at Clayton's direction, appointed Barbour and Ragland to the same jobs.

Both factions sent teams rushing back to Little Rock to lobby Hadley. Downs, a Mason ally, gave up quickly, and Barbour became the assessor, although he is not named as such in a list of Chicot County officials of the period. Possibly unable to sort through the confusion, an Arkansas historian omitted the entire slate of county officers for 1870–72. The dispute between Ragland and Mason went on until August, when Ragland finally resigned from a post he had never actually held. After months of turmoil, the appointed slate of Chicot County officials finally assumed their posts.[11]

Barbour found no peace in his victory, however, because many Arkansans resented men like Barbour who gained visibility and office as recent arrivals to the state. Barbour was now a county official and a former legislator with experience in business and race politics. He had come a long way since his days as a riverboat steward in Louisville. Yet none of these accomplishments mattered to conservatives, whose newspaper belittled Barbour in a gossipy article in May.

As conflict raged over the county appointments in Chicot, the *Arkansas Gazette* ran a story intended to humiliate him. Describing Barbour as a "carpet-bagger" and "sharp mulatto," the paper said he was former restaurant keeper who had gone bankrupt in Alton. "Having no money, but much cheek," the paper said, he came to Arkansas to try politics. "So neatly did he manage matters," he was soon a member of the legislature. Barbour's appointment in Lake Village had the "irate Africans" of the county "ready for war." The *Gazette* demanded invocation of the Grant administration's Force Bill to stop the "black ku-klux" in Chicot County from bringing disorder. An impudent servant who gained election by a sort of neat, sinister guile, Barbour was so odious, according to the paper, that even local blacks would not tolerate him.[12]

Pressing its attack two days later, the *Gazette* quoted a Louisville paper identifying Barbour as a "bootblack" on the steamer *Fashion* twenty years earlier, around 1851. "He [Barbour] once challenged Jim Steward, another airy darkey, to fight a duel because the cream-colored chamber-maid" chose Steward over Barbour. "Jim couldn't see it, and they didn't fight," the story said. The article was meant to insult Barbour further and incite white readers. Not a successful steamboat steward, but a shoeshine boy, Barbour arrogantly sought a duel—a white gentlemen's game—with another man over a light-skinned woman. His opponent, although being another "airy darkey," showed better sense by refusing the challenge.[13]

These were unfair distortions of Barbour and his history. A taxpaying resident of Louisville in the late 1840s and early 1850s, he was more than a former bootblack on the steamboats. Gibson remembered Conway as a prominent steward in Louisville's African American community when he wrote his memoir fifty years after their friendship. Barbour was proud, as was evident in his letters to Governor Yates in 1863. The attribute, esteemed in white society, was considered pretentious in a black man. Unwilling to credit Barbour's accomplishments, the paper used tidbits gleaned from other sources to malign him. By these means and others, Conservatives sought to curtail black political advancement in Reconstruction Arkansas.

Historians Glenn C. Altschuler and Stuart M. Blumin used newspapers as sources in arguing that Americans' absorption with politics in the nineteenth century has been exaggerated. The extraordinarily high level of participation in national elections after 1840 was, in their view, the result of the work of small, but effective, groups of party activists who turned out the vote on election day. Otherwise, they argued, most Americans were concerned with their daily existence and were virtually apolitical in between the quadrennial national contests. Critics of this argument point to the large numbers of newspapers published in the United States in the nineteenth century and their overwhelmingly political nature. Historian Mark Neely, commenting on the Altschuler-Blumin thesis, quoted the head of the federal census bureau as saying that 80 percent of the country's newspapers in 1860 were "political in their character." Newspapers owed their solvency to the ongoing interest in politics of an American public that evaluated candidates and issues not only during national elections but in "odd and even years alike."[14]

If we are to judge Reconstruction politics through newspapers, the *Gazette*'s article on Barbour shows how ugly they had become in Arkansas by the early 1870s. Catering to its racist, white Democratic readership, the paper's attack on Barbour demonstrated that black Republicans were to receive no quarter. In their anger at black political empowerment, the

Gazette's editors employed all the racial ammunition they could muster to defame him. As we shall see, the paper's ire was not directed at Barbour solely but at all "airy darkeys" who allied with the Republicans.

Barbour did not respond to the attacks but, instead, continued to expand his portfolio. He asked for and received credentials as an attorney from Associate Justice E. J. Searle of the Arkansas Supreme Court after supplying the Clayton ally with "satisfactory evidence of his good moral character and qualification." Barbour was certified to practice in the supreme and all inferior courts in the state. He swore his oath the last day of September 1871; the clerk of the state supreme court recorded his license the following February. Barbour's rival for tax assessor had been a lawyer, and although Downs had relinquished his claim to the county job, Barbour, possibly anticipating more trouble, acquired the means to counter further legal challenges to his position and a new way to make money. With the stroke of Searle's pen, Barbour became a lawyer, one of only three black attorneys in Lake Village during the period.[15]

Less than two months after he swore his oath, Barbour bought four town lots in Lake Village from Charles H. Carlton, a former officer in the Confederate Army, for $955. The full amount was due by 1 March 1872; thereafter, interest accumulated on the note at 2 percent per month. As security, Barbour sold Carlton all of his household goods, including a piano, for $5, the sale being void when Barbour paid off the lots. The presence of a piano, the symbol of middle-class refinement, among his belongings suggests a financial stability he did not enjoy. His property in both Cleveland and Alton had been auctioned off only a few months before, and despite his county job and newly acquired legal credentials in Arkansas, Barbour paid the debt to Carlton a full eighteen months later than agreed. Even so, with his large Lake Village homestead, license to practice law, and county office, Barbour accumulated the trappings of an important resident of Chicot County.[16]

―――――――

The political atmosphere in the county remained tense, however, because Republicans, many of them northern-born whites, controlled local offices, a fact that produced conflict with native men, elite and otherwise. Sheriff Walker was from New York, as was the county treasurer, J. E. Joslyn. County Clerk H. W. Graves was born in Vermont. Native black Republican H. Clark was the coroner; Mason, the county judge. Barbour, a black Republican "carpetbagger," was offensive for all three attributes. Many of

Chicot County's white residents resented the presence of outsiders and their black friends in county politics. They also opposed the tax levies Republicans put in place to fund development projects.[17]

A bond issue to support railroad construction brought these racial and economic tensions to a violent climax a short while later, putting Chicot County's "trouble" in the pages of newspapers across the nation. In January 1871 and again late in the year, Chicot County voters were asked to approve $200,000 in bonds for two railroads. The measure was approved in both elections, but both times Republican officials allowed transient railroad laborers to vote as county residents. Chicot County Democrats opposed the bonds, the tax support they required, and the fraud employed to manipulate the elections' outcomes. They also understood that Mason had demanded a $10,000 bribe from the railroad companies for his support of the bond issue and the votes he delivered in its favor. For conservatives, the bond issue epitomized Republican corruption and their own powerlessness.[18]

Wathal Wynn, a young black attorney, paid the price for this white frustration. Wynn, only recently arrived in Lake Village and possibly Mason's brother-in-law, helped Mason shepherd the vote for the railroad bill. Born in Virginia, Wynn graduated from Howard University with a law degree early in 1871. He was admitted to the bar in Washington, DC, shortly thereafter, and to Hustings Circuit Court in Richmond, Virginia, in March, making him Virginia's first black lawyer. When he received credentials to practice law in Arkansas in September, Wynn became the first black lawyer in the country licensed to practice in three jurisdictions.[19]

For some Chicot County whites, however, Wynn was a coconspirator in the tainted elections and Mason's extortion of the railroad companies. On 11 December, a few weeks after the second vote on the railroad bonds, Wynn and a few others had dinner at Mason's home, near the county courthouse in Lake Village. After dinner, Wynn stopped at a grocery store owned by Curtis Garrett, who had been in trouble with the Freedman's Bureau for his involvement in an attack on a bureau agent's home and for "mistreating a freedman." John H. Saunders, cited by the bureau for failing to honor labor contracts with local blacks, and Jasper Dugan were also in the store. Reportedly, both Wynn and Saunders were drunk. The two men got into an argument over the railroad bonds, and Saunders stabbed Wynn in the neck, killing him. The three white men were arrested and jailed.[20]

The response to Wynn's murder reinforced white fears about the dangers of an empowered African American community. When word of the murder got out, Chicot County blacks, mustering up as the "Sons of Africa," forced Sheriff Walker to give up the keys to the jail—now found—and on Friday, 15 December, took the three white men out of the jail and "shot, beat, and mangled" their bodies. The black mob, numbering about three hundred, spent the next several days pillaging, looting, and demanding money from Saunders's family members. According to the *Gazette*, which probably exaggerated the extent of the rioting, terrified whites fled the county in great numbers.[21]

Throughout the South, interpretations of what was happening in Chicot County revealed the persistent racial divide. On one side, white southerners, told of armed blacks on the rampage, were ready to mobilize. The Memphis Chamber of Commerce discussed plans to send a contingent that would place itself "at the disposal" of the Chicot County sheriff. Nathan Bedford Forrest, the former Confederate general and founder of the Ku Klux Klan, said he was willing, personally, to "speedily restore order." On the other side, Memphis blacks were said to be arming themselves and heading south to aid the African Americans. Fearing an escalation of the violence, Governor Hadley sent Adjutant General D. H. Danforth to assess the situation in Chicot on 21 December.[22]

Violence was a political tool in the South throughout the entire Reconstruction period, almost always white-on-black violence. Therefore, the lynching of the three white men in Chicot was, as Foner described it, "indeed a rare occurrence." More commonly, whites convinced other whites that blacks were about to attack them and that a preemptive strike was necessary, as happened repeatedly in Mississippi. Democratic leaders, complaining about Republican taxes and corruption, tried to distance themselves from the violence, but they often sponsored or sanctioned the racist paramilitary groups that committed atrocities. Blacks who sought to defend themselves gave their opponents an excuse for more violence. That is what happened in Colfax, Louisiana, "the bloodiest single instance of racial carnage in the Reconstruction era." In Colfax, the seat of Grant Parish, a black-majority parish, African Americans were murdered outright in a fight, ostensibly over who would be sheriff, but more accurately over white supremacy. All told, almost three hundred blacks were slaughtered in Colfax on Easter Sunday in 1873, many behind a white flag of surrender. Colfax was the most brutal incident of white-on-black violence during Reconstruction, but it was typical in that whites were the aggressors. The lynching by blacks of the three white men in Chicot was an anomaly, but it played into the hands of white supremacists who could point to Lake

Village as proof that only slavery had kept blacks' murderous tendencies in check.[23]

Recognizing the inflammatory nature of events and the possible repercussions, Barbour, a witness to the "Chicot County Trouble," tried to underplay the seriousness of the conflict when he arrived in Little Rock on Monday, Christmas Day. He told *Gazette* editors, who interviewed him the next day, that law enforcement was in complete control in Lake Village and that "no depredations" had been committed when he left Chicot County the previous Friday. Although plenty of depredations had taken place, Barbour's assertion of increased order was affirmed by accounts published elsewhere. Barbour minimized the crisis to reassure panicked whites seeing their worst fears being realized in Chicot County, but he was also engaging in politics. Barbour and Sheriff Walker were allied against Mason. Barbour therefore had a stake in saying that Walker had matters under control, particularly since Mason was widely believed to have instigated the violence against the prisoners. In a letter to Washington calling for martial law throughout the South, Mason, "bowed in sorrow," described the killing of Wynn without ever mentioning the subsequent murders of Saunders, Garrett, and Jasper, whom he called "ku-klux assassins." Many people thought Mason was responsible for the killings, and Barbour sought to capitalize on that perception.[24]

A show of force by the state and national governments brought the crisis to a close, but the memory of the Sons of Africa haunted white Chicot County for years. To ensure order, Governor Hadley sent a contingent of the governor's guards, and the federal government dispatched troops from New Orleans in early 1872. By mid-April, the troops were withdrawn, and the Chicot County Trouble was over, or so it appeared. County Democrats never forgot the murders of the white men and the violence perpetrated by enraged blacks. After the state legislature restored voting rights to former Confederates in 1873, Mason was tried and convicted for his part in the "massacre." He was released on a writ of habeas corpus and served no time. Some years after Mason's death, vengeful Democrats indicted Mason's white allies in Chicot County, seeking belated justice. Extant editions of the *Lake Shore Sentinel* document the court proceedings and the vigorous rehashing of the events in 1871.[25]

For Barbour, the Chicot County Trouble created new political possibilities and a new alliance. In March, Abram W. Shadd, Wathal Wynn's classmate at Howard University, arrived in Lake Village. Shadd, brother of newspaper editor Mary Ann Shadd Cary, had been friends with Wynn while the two were in law school. After Wynn's murder, Shadd, who also practiced law across the river in Washington County, Mississippi, was licensed in Chicot, primarily to settle Wynn's estate. An entry in the 1865 Madison County census for an "A. Shadd" in Alton suggests that Barbour may have met Shadd after the latter's service in the Civil War. The two men apparently worked together; Chicot County court records show both Barbour and Shadd filing claims against Mason's estate after he died in 1874. Mason was alive and well in 1872, however, and Barbour, believing his rival was now vulnerable, decided to challenge Mason in a race for sheriff.[26]

The contest took place within the broader context of the Brooks-Baxter war, the contentious and confusing gubernatorial contest in 1872 that also marked the beginning of Arkansas's "redemption." Paradoxically, the divisive Clayton, most closely associated with the state's Reconstruction, can be credited with planting the seeds for its demise. Clayton's fickle use of patronage was not limited to the appointments in Chicot County. His shifting allegiances produced enemies and friends who soon became enemies. The accumulation of opponents put Arkansas back in the hands of Democrats in 1874, but the problems had begun several years earlier.

A Clayton ally, Joseph Brooks, had helped Clayton become governor in 1868, in part by keeping the voting booths open beyond the appointed closing times. Expecting some share of the spoils, Brooks was disappointed when Claytonites failed to nominate him for the seat he wanted in the U.S. House of Representatives. Brooks harbored a grudge and lay in wait as Governor Hadley's term came to an end. In early 1872, Brooks and other unhappy Republicans formed a splinter group within the party called "brindletails" to counter Clayton's so-called minstrels. The brindletails were Liberal Republicans who wanted universal amnesty and suffrage, meaning full political rights for former Confederates, a direct appeal for Democratic support. The faction's nickname arose from a black man's comment that Brooks's voice reminded him of an old mule. Clayton's followers were called minstrels because one of them, Jon Price, editor of the *Little Rock Republican*, had once been a member of a minstrel group. Although Brooks hoped to attract African American partisans, the racial connotations of the Claytonites' moniker likely helped him with Democrats. Since the sitting governor, Hadley, had been only an interim choice, Senator Clayton and his supporters chose Elisha Baxter, a Virginia native who had lived in Arkansas since 1852, as their nominee, hoping that he would appeal to the homegrown despite Clayton's backing.[27]

Although Barbour was an experienced campaign speaker, he received blistering reviews when he went on the stump that spring to defend his wing of the party and its gubernatorial candidate. He spoke on Baxter's behalf at a political rally in Monticello in nearby Drew County in April. Brooks and a supporter, John Williams, were soliciting votes in a brindle-tail-friendly area; Barbour and another black man represented the Clay-tonites. Williams addressed the crowd first, attacking the Clayton-Hadley regime as "statehouse swindlers." Barbour's response began with an ad hominem attack on Williams and deteriorated from there. He mistakenly put Camden in Hempstead County (it is in Ouachita); said all state-funded track for the Mississippi, Ouachita, and Red River Railroad was laid (also untrue); and called the brindletails "thieves and scoundrels," among many other comments. When Brooks took the podium, he called Barbour a liar, although most of his attacks were aimed at Clayton. The *Gazette* ridiculed Barbour's performance and said he interrupted Brooks repeatedly, "belching forth obnoxious oaths." Humbled by Brooks's scorching answers and "withering sarcasms," Barbour was said to have abandoned the campaign and returned to Lake Village. The *Gazette*, which had previously slandered Barbour, was biased, and Barbour probably did not embarrass himself to the extent it alleged. Still, he did not, apparently, again speak on Baxter's behalf and instead turned his attention to his contest with Mason for sheriff and control of Chicot County.[28]

The Conservative newspaper happily reported this battle between the two African American politicians, if only to highlight the problems within the Republican Party. The *Gazette*'s editors liked neither man, although the paper had once favorably compared the former state senator to his General Assembly compeers, including Barbour. The paper described their competition in August, saying Mason was presumed to carry the black vote of Chicot "in his capacious pantaloons." And so he did until Barbour, "another sable gentleman," appeared on the scene. A rivalry between the two men had been growing for more than a year. Mason claimed to be "master of the colored vote—Barbour disputed it, setting himself up as leader." Both were Clayton men, but that had not precluded the rupture in Chicot County. Whereas competition among white politicians was expected as a part of vigorous civic discourse, for the racist *Gazette* the struggle between these two black politicians was further evidence of their inappropriate participation in the public sphere. The paper, therefore, diligently reported the details of their ongoing squabble.

The *Gazette* was particularly interested when Chicot County Republicans held a convention to choose delegates for the state convention in anticipation of the fall gubernatorial elections, and the rivalry between Mason and Barbour became violent. According to the paper, the county was about evenly split between the two, and, anticipating trouble, each side armed its men. There were two gatherings in Lake Village that August: Judge Mason and his backers met inside the county courthouse; Barbour and his followers clustered outside in the yard. When "it occurred to Barbour's convention that Mason was getting the best of them," the assessor and his supporters went into the courthouse to "see how it was." A gun battled ensued, and one of Barbour's supporters, Jack White, was killed. At the end of the day, the *Gazette* explained, both Barbour and Mason were nominated as county sheriff and were leading separate delegations to the Republican state convention. The editors referred derisively to the clash as the "War of the Roses."[29]

Violence or the threat of it had been central to Barbour's political experience in Arkansas since his service in the legislature. As one of Clayton's top Invincibles, Barbour had promised, but had not been compelled to deliver, martial support of the governor. Physically threatened on his first visit to Lake Village, Barbour had retreated until then-governor Hadley confirmed his appointment as tax assessor. When the Chicot County Trouble erupted, Barbour fled to Little Rock, where he assured the *Gazette* that things were not as bad as they seemed. Beyond the *Gazette's* assertion that he had once sought a duel, little evidence suggests that Barbour desired physical confrontation with anyone, much less the shootout described by the paper. If he had tested his manhood years earlier on the rivers, by 1872, Barbour, in his early fifties, was an unlikely combatant despite his political ambitions. The violent nature of Chicot County politics, therefore, put him at a disadvantage to Mason, who was younger, a native, and, as Barbour declared, experienced in the art of mob action.

In an exchange of letters to the editors of the *Gazette*, both Barbour and Mason presented themselves as the rightful face of Chicot County Republicanism and blamed each other for the death of Jack White. Barbour said he had the support of the county's Republican executive committee and went into the courthouse only to inform Mason of that fact. Mason's men opened fire and killed White, thereby bringing an end to the meeting inside the courthouse, although Barbour's meeting outside continued. Mason disputed Barbour's assertion of an endorsement by the executive committee, arguing that he and his guests constituted the

Republican Party in Chicot County. Mason argued that White was undoubtedly killed by Barbour's people, and he invited readers to ask any "unbiased conservative or republican, white or black" about the truthfulness of his version. Barbour, in a retort, said, "I have never led a mob in my life, while Mr. Mason has gotten up a number in Chicot county since my residence there." And everybody knew it. "Every time he has had a political contest, as is well known, he has had an armed force to back him, and to intimidate his opponents," Barbour said. He concluded by saying that, since Mason's statements were untrue and "not worth further notice," he would not trouble the editors again.[30]

The conflict between two black Republicans entertained the editors of the *Gazette*, but it left unresolved which man would get the support of Arkansas's state Republican Party. The answer came shortly. Black Republican politicians in Arkansas were charged foremost with delivering votes at election time, and Mason, the native, was perceived by the state party as the better vote getter in his home area. Barbour, the outsider, had exceeded his usefulness as a Republican operative. Just as the Clayton faction had abandoned Joseph Brooks, Major Ragland, and Frank Downs, it now discarded Barbour, no longer an asset to the faltering Clayton wing of the Arkansas Republican Party.

Barbour discovered the truth later that month when the Republican convention, or "Minstrel Conclave" as the *Gazette* called it, gathered in Little Rock. Both Barbour's and Mason's delegations sought to be recognized as the legitimate representatives of Republican Chicot County. The credentials committee considered the two slates but reported in Mason's favor. Barbour would not quit. He "arose and wanted to know if contestants were to have no rights," but members said that, since Barbour was not a recognized delegate, he could not address the convention. The assessor persisted despite being shouted down repeatedly. James Barton, Clayton's former secretary who had been so instrumental in putting Barbour in the legislature in 1871, tried to speak on Barbour's behalf, but the request fell on deaf ears. By a large majority, the convention adopted the committee report choosing Mason's slate. A headline in the *Gazette* said, "Conway Barbour's Delegation from Chicot Overboard."[31]

Thrown into the metaphorical abyss, an embittered Barbour told a *Gazette* reporter, "They [Clayton men] are a d—d set of scoundrels. They have no use for any man they cannot use." The statement, despite its circular nature, revealed Barbour's frustration. From his point of view, the Republicans' failure to seat him and his friends instead of the Mason ticket constituted betrayal of the highest order. Barbour stuck by Clayton through impeachment and beyond and was a second lieutenant in the governor's military squad. Barbour both overestimated his importance to the Claytonites and underestimated Mason's political agility and ruthlessness.[32]

In the blood sport that constituted Arkansas's Reconstruction politics, Mason demonstrated his talents again in the fall when he and his friends contrived to throw out the votes in three Chicot County precincts. Candidates for office, they proclaimed themselves election judges but then disqualified themselves because they were also office seekers. Because they had been both candidates and election judges, the votes in the precincts could be disqualified. This was "a put up job," intended to benefit the top of the state ticket. If gubernatorial candidate Joseph Brooks, whom they opposed, won the election, the victory could be contested on the basis of their erstwhile conflict of interest. If Elisha Baxter, whom they supported, became governor, the result could not be challenged successfully because they had eliminated the conflict. It was brilliant, complex gamesmanship of the political system and suggested the degree to which Barbour, new to this level of politics, was no match for them.[33]

An embittered Barbour then watched as Clayton's missteps help put Arkansas back into the hands of conservatives, men dedicated to reversing the Republican policies for which Barbour had fought. The Republican descent began with apparent victory when Clayton's man, Baxter, defeated Brooks in the gubernatorial election in November 1872. Brooks lost, but not solidly and in part because of the corrupt election system he himself created four years earlier to benefit Clayton. Brooks claimed fraud—which he certainly recognized—and waited for the courts to validate his victory. Once in office, Baxter betrayed the Clayton wing by courting conservatives. He appointed men of both parties to office and supported a franchise bill in 1873 that restored political privileges to former Confederates. He also refused to support Claytonite-sponsored legislation in the General Assembly, thereby earning a reputation as an independent man of virtue among Democrats. His support among "radical" Republicans, however, declined in equal measure.[34]

Baxter's apostasy soon convinced Republicans that he had to be removed from office. Dozens of legislators had resigned their seats to take better-paying jobs in Baxter's state government, and when Democrats won a small majority in the special election held to fill those slots, Republicans were frantic. To reverse the results of the election, they first needed to remove Baxter, their own candidate only a short time earlier. The only way to do it was by coup d'état.[35]

In April 1874, a pliant local judge ruled in favor of Brooks's old challenge to the 1872 election results and proclaimed him governor. Chief Justice McClure of the state supreme court, unsuccessfully impeached back in 1871, swore in Brooks on the spot. The new "governor," backed by a contingent of military men, burst into Baxter's office and demanded that he relinquish his position. When Baxter refused, he was dragged from the premises. Around the same time, Brooks's men seized the state militia arsenal in Little Rock. By midday, some three hundred armed men occupied the state capital, and both sides began wiring President Grant seeking support. Grant initially supported Brooks, and Clayton sent word to his former ally, then opponent, and now ally again, to hold firm.[36]

The coup began to fall apart, however, when Baxter, who was briefly jailed but released, set up his own headquarters near the capital. He wired Grant for help, declared martial law in Little Rock's Pulaski County, and called on the people to support him. Skirmishes between his people and the Brooks army produced casualties but no definitive result.[37]

Now confronted with a miniature civil war in Little Rock, Grant wired both Brooks and Baxter, denying each use of the arsenal and suggesting they let the courts settle the dispute. That was easier said than done. At one point, two state supreme court justices, including the man who had given Barbour his legal credentials, were kidnapped to prevent them from ruling on who should be in the governor's mansion. In the end, the federal government supported Baxter, and faced with the prospect of federal troops, Brooks gave up.

President Grant's decision to support Baxter "sealed the doom of Arkansas Reconstruction." The victorious Baxter rewarded his loyalists, many of them Democrats, and in late 1874, the "mastermind" of his strategy, Democrat Augustus Garland, won election as Arkansas governor. It would be almost a century before a Republican again held that office.[38]

The Brooks-Baxter war and the subsequent end of Reconstruction in Arkansas can be traced in large measure to Clayton's erratic loyalties as the state's Republican boss. Unable to control Baxter, Clayton turned on him and set in motion a series of events that resulted in a return to power of Arkansas's prewar landholding elite. The Democrats, primarily concerned with financial matters, did not immediately seek to undo the progress that African Americans had achieved in Arkansas during Reconstruction; Garland was a moderate on race relations. As C. Vann Woodward argued, Jim

Crow came later when propertied whites were threatened with Populist cohesion across racial boundaries. African Americans continued to hold office and have access to public accommodations, although often segregated, under the state's 1873 civil rights law. Still, just as Grant's affirmation of Baxter was a turning point on the road to redemption, the return to power of Democrats and their need to garner rural support eventually produced racially restrictive legislation and Jim Crow.[39]

———

For Barbour, the prolonged dispute over the outcome of the 1872 gubernatorial election paled in importance to his own failure to become sheriff and wrest political control of Chicot County from James Mason. His future in jeopardy, Barbour pressed his case with letters to the Little Rock newspaper. In January 1873, fresh from the loss, Barbour sent the *Gazette* a long missive vilifying both Mason and former governor Hadley as corrupt men who had conspired against him. Before the fall election, Barbour said, then-governor Hadley tried to force Barbour to drop out of the sheriff's race and support Mason. Hadley told him that "Mason might become desperate, and that there might not be as many men to vote" on election day as there were that day; in other words, Mason might kill Barbour if he did not give up his challenge. This was a very serious charge and creditable when one considers Mason's history. Barbour undermined its strength, however, by following the allegation with mundane complaints about Mason's partisan appointments. Barbour, it appears, was less concerned for his health than for his diminished stature. He sought intervention by new-governor Baxter, who, unbeknown to Barbour but like him, was about to be abandoned by the Claytonites.[40]

Although Barbour complained strenuously about Hadley and Mason, he never mentioned Clayton, who had put Hadley in the governor's office and whose minions had chosen Mason over Barbour at the 1872 convention. Clayton, who controlled Arkansas's Republicans from afar, had probably sent Hadley to deliver the death threat, but Barbour did not realize it. Although he complained to the *Gazette* about scoundrels in the Republican Party, Barbour remained personally loyal to Clayton, even as Clayton and his supporters left Barbour to fend for himself in Chicot County.

Financial setbacks exacerbated Barbour's political frustrations. Tax records for McConnell Township in 1873 show that he owned two horses, two cows, and three hogs, as well as a "pleasure carriage," two gold or silver watches, and a pianoforte. His tax bill on this property, amounting to a little more than $12, is listed as paid. Nonetheless, other records indicate he was again in financial straits, and in good company, as the country reeled from a recession so deep that some Americans referred to it as the "Great Depression" until the deeper financial trough of the 1930s.[41]

In transactions reminiscent of his years in Alton, Barbour contrived to remain solvent, using whomever and whatever he could. His mother-in-law, Matilda Rankin, underwrote the purchase of land formerly owned by one of the men murdered during the Chicot County Trouble. The Barbours were unable to fulfill the terms of the deal, and a confused, messy lawsuit ended up before the Arkansas Supreme Court in 1880, four years after Conway's death, with his mother-in-law and wife getting nothing and Conway posthumously implicated in fraud. In 1873, Barbour obtained Mrs. Rankins's power of attorney in order to recoup any assets she might have owned in Louisville. Trying to protect his Chicot County holdings, Barbour deeded his Lake Village lots to Frances. He took whatever he could get from legal clients in lieu of cash: mules from Jerry Carson, an illiterate black laborer, for a debt of $250; a horse from John Bird, who owed Barbour $75.[42]

These transactions were simple compared to the labyrinth of deed transfers involving the donation lands Barbour acquired shortly after leaving the legislature. He owed $144.80 in back taxes on the acreage, which he paid in April 1875, right before he sold 1,200 acres to Henry McPike of Alton for $1,200. The following month, Frances bought 1,500 acres of Chicot County land from L. H. Springer, but the description of the land is virtually identical to that which the Barbours had just sold to McPike. A few days later, Conway and Frances sold one hundred acres of the same land to Prince Princeton, of Chicot County, for $100 cash. Finally, the Barbours sold (or resold) the land to their friend Henry Basse, the man who had financed Barbour's businesses in Alton.[43]

This tangled web of financial transactions was typical of Barbour's economic life. He had left Louisville with sufficient means to become a homeowner in Cleveland. In Alton, he had purchased property outright in 1859 but then mortgaged, quitclaimed, and manipulated his assets into ruin. In Lake Village, the Illinois pattern reemerged as professional and personal setbacks took him from seeming stability to panicked reorganization.

As if Barbour were not troubled enough with professional and financial problems, in 1874, the Mississippi River came out of its banks, flooding Chicot County and most of the southern delta. The inundation reached enormous and alarming proportions by mid-April. More than 8 million acres of Louisiana, 2.5 million acres of Mississippi, and 2 million acres of Arkansas, including all of Chicot County, were underwater in May. The mayor of New Orleans, chairman and treasurer of the General Relief Committee, made a plea to the rest of the country on 30 May 1874, begging for help with the present emergency and the famine he anticipated when the waters finally subsided.

The commissioner of relief from Boston, who visited the area, said "the calamity surpasses in extent and ruinous consequences any that has occurred from fire, storm or flood on this continent in the current century." The $3 million in levee bonds issued by Arkansas's Republicans had produced fifty-three miles of levee construction, but much of the work lacked quality. Even the best-constructed levees did not withstand the magnitude of the flooding. Nature seemed to be conspiring against residents of the Arkansas delta, black and white.[44]

Chicot County's predominately black population suffered another blow even as water levels slowly began to fall. In June, the Freedman's Savings Bank defaulted, depriving the local blacks of their meager savings and prompting Barbour to accept livestock in lieu of cash. For financial and personal reasons, Barbour also tried to get money from Mason's estate.

Barbour had previously demonstrated a willingness to skirt the edges of legality and propriety in his dealings, and he did so again after Mason, who was still sheriff despite being a convicted murderer, died in November 1874. Surprisingly, Barbour and Frank Downs, who succeeded Mason as county judge, witnessed the dead man's will, although the appearance of the ink in the will book suggests their names were added later. Mason left everything to his wife, Marie. In April 1875, the county court issued a citation against Barbour demanding that he "show cause why he detained and concealed certain property" belonging to Mason's estate. He was ordered to deliver the unnamed property to the administrator forthwith. Barbour was one of many people, including Shadd, who filed claims against the Mason estate. The amount of Barbour's claim is blank in the court record. On 14 October 1875, the court denied the claim and Barbour's request for a new trial. Barbour intended to appeal, but he never got the chance.[45]

Conclusion

ON 8 JULY 1876, the *Gazette* announced, "Conway Barbour, an old colored lawyer, and formerly a favorite servant of Gov. Barbour, of Kentucky, died in Lake Village a short time ago." A Cincinnati paper reported his death about two weeks later. "For ten years past a prominent colored politician and officeholder," Barbour was also remembered as a steward on the *Eclipse* and other fine Ohio River boats. Chicot County has no death certificate or probate record to help illuminate the circumstances of his passing, and the entire 1876 run of the *Alton Telegraph*, which would have run a detailed obituary, burned in a fire. Many of his family members are buried together in an Upper Alton cemetery, and he might be buried there too, but he is not listed in the cemetery's record book. Like his earliest years, his last year leaves us with many unanswered—and possibly unanswerable—questions.[1]

What we do know of him suggests that an aspiring black middle class was trying to take shape alongside its white counterpart in the middle of the nineteenth century. In each place Barbour lived, we find that he and others like him were pursuing opportunities and seeking to better themselves vocationally and economically, seeking respectability and stature in their communities. In Louisville, as William Gibson described, the best opportunities were on the river. Stewards, like Barbour and the Rankin brothers, and other boatmen, while not wealthy like businessman Washington Spradling, were prominent in the community and lived comfortably in their homes. The river gave them the chance to broaden their horizons, so that when Barbour learned of the emigration convention in Cleveland in 1854, he took advantage of the opportunity. There, he met men like Martin Delany, H. Ford Douglas, John Mercer Langston, and John Malvin, all of whom, like Barbour, relocated repeatedly in search of better fortune. In Alton, Barbour's neighbors—Isaac Kelly, Reverend R. J. Robinson, H. D. King, Edward White, C. C. Richardson, and others—

were small-business owners who, like Barbour, participated in politics and, unlike him, were active in church and fraternal organizations. When the Union Depot failed, Barbour returned south, creating an employment and land agency and making contacts that would help put him in the legislature.

In each location, Barbour ingratiated himself with white allies. In Louisville, Captain Monroe Quarrier, boat pilot Robert Bell, the Ratels, and Aristide Vatble helped Conway and Cornelia manage as free blacks in a slave society. J. Ingersoll helped him out in Cleveland; Henry Basse financed his businesses in Alton and lent him money against properties in Ohio and Arkansas. Barbour reached out—unsuccessfully—to Illinois governor Richard Yates. In Arkansas, Governor Powell Clayton helped make him one of only about six hundred African American state legislators elected during Reconstruction in the United States and appointed him to what should have been a sinecure in Lake Village. Arkansas Supreme Court justice E. J. Searle made him a lawyer with a pen stroke. Ironically, it was another mulatto, James W. Mason, who denied Barbour the sheriff's office and leadership of Chicot County's black Republicans. Both Barbour and Mason were born to wealthy white families, but Mason had advantages that Barbour did not.

As we have seen, Barbour skirted the edge of propriety when necessary. His tangled business dealings and manipulation of properties were common features of nineteenth-century financial transactions. His bigamy, willingness to defraud Western Transit Insurance, and apparent involvement in a kidnapping were not. A property case brought before the Arkansas Supreme Court four years after Barbour's death showed that he had been dishonest even with his mother-in-law, Matilda Rankin. Violence, however, was not in his nature. On many occasions, he absented himself when things got hot. He liked being associated with Clayton's Invincibles, but one imagines he was relieved that he did not actually have to battle. He did not want to fight in the Civil War; he wanted to recruit others to do it.[2]

Barbour was blessed with intelligence, personal competence, and energy. Lacking formal education, he educated himself. His letters to Illinois governor Richard Yates in 1863 were full of errors, unlike those written in the early 1870s to the Arkansas paper. He was quick to identify opportunities as they appeared, in personal relationships, business, and politics. He relocated repeatedly in pursuit of a better situation. In short, he used all the tools in his tool kit to try to build a better life.

Barbour's family absorbed his middle-class values, aspirations, and assumptions. He fathered sixteen children between 1845 and 1875, seven by Cornelia and nine by Frances. Unable to leave them much in terms of a financial inheritance, Barbour bequeathed tools—intelligence, ambition, and pride—that are apparent in what we can find of the family's history.

Four of Barbour's daughters—one by Cornelia and three by Frances—were involved in legal battles defending their livelihoods and citizenship. One of those suits involved Julia, born 25 September 1861 in Alton. Like many of her sisters, she was a teacher. In the early 1890s, she was teaching in Cairo, Illinois. In the 1892–93 school year, Julia was teacher and principal of second and fourth graders in the city's Garrison School.

In May 1893, Julia received a letter from Theodore W. Jones of Provident Hospital and Training School for Nurses asking if she was planning on attending the World's Fair in Chicago. The hospital had decided to combine the positions of clerk and matron, and Jones thought Julia might be interested in the job, which he described as "something better than that of teaching school." The hospital's founder, Dr. Daniel Hale Williams, was interested in meeting her if and when she visited Chicago. Julia replied that she was undecided about visiting the fair but provided Jones with a catalogue of Cairo schools. Since Provident initiated the correspondence, she presumed that letters regarding her "competency, integrity, etc., will be unnecessary." Jones responded with an offer of $6 a week, including expenses: "this means board, room, and laundry."[3]

Writing from her mother's home in Alton on 12 June, Julia said the salary offered was "less than I can accept." She countered that she might be willing to remove herself from the cares of the classroom, however, if the position were for a "considerable length of time at a salary of thirty dollars per month." She needed an answer quickly, so as to give the Cairo Board of Education time to replace her. When Provident offered her one year's employment at $24 per month and $30 per month thereafter, she balked. Train fare alone would eat up a chunk of her first year's salary, she wrote. "Had I some assurance . . . that I would be retained, say for two or three years . . . then I would at once accept," she said.

On 17 June, Jones replied that if she could promise good behavior, "not engage in piques and quarrels with the nurses," and "render honest and intelligent service," she could consider herself employed for three years and probably longer. She started the job on 19 June 1893 but was discharged on 5 January 1894, when her position was eliminated "owing to the stringency of the times." She sued for breach of contract and won a judgment of $621 on 27 November 1894. Provident Hospital appealed the verdict and lost in March 1895. The court noted that Julia had been unable to find employment after being fired, but that probably had more to do with her health than her reputation. She died of tuberculosis on 12 July 1895 at age thirty-three. She did not get to enjoy her vindication, but she died having successfully fought back against powerful men who had misled her and snatched away her livelihood.[4]

A decade earlier, Josephine, or Josie, Cornelia and Conway's second daughter, was also involved in a lawsuit after being discriminated against by a Chicago theatre. Born in Louisville in May 1854, Josie married a barber, John T. Curry, on 12 March 1883, in Chicago. Like her sister, Catherine (Kate Diggs), Josie Curry was often mentioned in the social columns of the *Western Appeal*. The paper praised her for inventing and marketing a product she called "Parisian Balm of Beauty" and kept track of folks who visited the Currys and whom the Currys visited.[5]

In June 1886, the Currys and two of John's employees from the barbershop decided to see a show at People's Theatre in Chicago. Josie tried to buy tickets for seats on the first balcony but was told that she and her group could not sit there because of their race. A white acquaintance bought the tickets for the foursome, but they were stopped before they could take the seats. An argument ensued. Josie testified that the manager, Josiah Baylies, threw money at her and shouted a racial slur. Josie sued the theatre for violating Illinois' Civil Rights Act of 1885, which outlawed discrimination in public accommodations. She won a $100 judgment after a one-day trial in March 1888. The verdict was upheld both by the appellate court and the Illinois Supreme Court the following year.[6]

While the case was ostensibly about racial discrimination, Josie's complaint centered more on class. She and her husband were successful and well connected. In addition to his barbershop, which he sold in October 1888, John Curry had a job in the municipal water department. They were—to use a charged term—respectable. They did not appreciate, therefore, being lumped in with all other African Americans. The Currys were not particularly active in Chicago's racial conversation, focused as they were on their own success. Josie's argument in the case, then, was more economic than racial: she thought she should be able to sit anywhere she could afford, a position her father would surely have supported.[7]

After John Curry died or left town in 1894, Josie married Samuel Alsup, a railroad porter and conductor. In 1900, Cornelia was living with them in Chicago; the former slave died three years later of pneumonia and a bad heart. Her death certificate listed her age as sixty-four years, although she was at least twenty years older. She is buried in Chicago's Oak Woods Cemetery. The Alsups appeared regularly in the pages of the *Chicago Defender* as Josie traveled to visit friends and family and bickered with her neighbors. After Samuel Alsup—"a man of sterling worth"—died on 2 October 1920, Josie disappeared, leaving only the complicated legacy of *Baylies v. Curry*.

Although they were not parties to the actual suit, a court case affecting Conway and Frances's daughters Fannie and Florence also suggests the complexities confronted by middle-class African Americans. Born fifteen years apart, Fannie in 1860 and Florence in 1875, the two sisters worked together as teachers in the Alton School District for many years. Alton schools had been integrated since the 1870s, but emboldened by nearby Upper Alton's refusal to comply with a state supreme court order to integrate and *Plessy v. Ferguson*, Alton's mayor, city council, and board of education decided to create separate primary schools for the city's black children in 1896–97. The high school, oddly, remained integrated. Two new "black schools," Lovejoy and Douglass, were built for the academic year commencing in fall 1897. When African American Scott Bibb's two children were turned away from the school they had previously attended and told they should go to Lovejoy instead, Bibb sued, and most African Americans began to boycott the new black schools.[8]

Fannie and Florence were among the four teachers hired to teach at the separate schools. Their cooperation with the city authorities angered others in the black community, and Florence did not help herself when she testified that, despite teaching at Lovejoy, she did not know it was a "colored school." Mother Frances and the two girls reportedly went door to door trying to convince black parents to send their children to the segregated schools. A critic warned Fannie that she and her mother should "go to the mirror . . . for they must have forgotten that they are Negroes by birth." The Barbours, in protecting their own economic interests, looked like "race-traitors" to their neighbors.[9]

Despite numerous court rulings in their favor, Alton's African Americans ultimately abandoned the boycott. City fathers simply would not comply with the court orders, and black parents reasoned that a separate education was better than none for their children. Fannie and Florence spent the rest of their careers teaching in Alton's separate black schools. Florence died in July 1918 from complications following goiter surgery, five years after her mother died. "One of the best known colored women in Alton," Florence, the newspaper said, chose the unpopular path of teaching for the segregated schools, but the black community, the writer alleged, eventually saw the wisdom of the board's decision. Her services had been so valuable that the school board paid her during her illness, even though everyone realized she would not return to work. Her sister Fannie died from diabetes on 8 May 1922. "Much beloved by her pupils," she "ranked high among the teachers of the city," the newspaper said.[10]

Julia's case against Provident Hospital, Josie's suit against People's Theatre, and Fannie and Florence's actions in the Alton school case demonstrate that their father's sense of pride, standing, and self-preservation did not die with him. More so than his sons, Barbour's daughters reflected his assumptions about the family's place in this country. Unfortunately, they did not have their own children to continue that legacy. With one exception, Barbour's sons and daughters died childless or had a single child who died young or childless.

Only Thomas, the child born to Conway and Frances in Louisville in 1848, has descendants, and they all go by Rankin since Thomas never took his father's name. In the 1860 Alton census, Thomas was a twelve-year-old schoolboy. A decade later, he was inaccurately listed in the census as age thirty-one (he was twenty-one), a boatman married to a Louisiana girl, Virginia Wright. It is not clear what happened to Thomas, but Virginia gave birth to his son, also named Thomas Conway Rankin, in Lake Village, Arkansas, on 16 April 1874, presumably with grandparents Conway and Frances Barbour at her side. Virginia Wright Rankin then married Alto Mitchell. The couple lived in Louisiana.[11]

Fifty years earlier, Conway Barbour was not long out of bondage. His grandson, Thomas Conway Rankin, went to college, graduating with a BA from New Orleans University in 1898. He married Carrie B. Kelsoe in 1900, and they raised many children. One of their daughters, Virginia (Virgie), was staying with her cousin Fannie in Alton according to the 1920 census. Thomas died 8 January 1942, after a career as a bookkeeper and stenographer. His descendants should know that their ancestor Conway Barbour fought like a tiger to make a better life for himself and his family and to contribute to his world in his time. He was one of countless—usually invisible—African Americans in the mid-nineteenth century grasping for their version of the American dream.[12]

APPENDIX

NOTES

BIBLIOGRAPHY

INDEX

Appendix: The Other Children

AS NOTED, CONWAY Barbour fathered sixteen children. The lives of four of those children are described in the conclusion. Below are some notes on the other twelve.

Mortality in the family was significant. Four of his children died as infants or as very small children. Lucien (born 1846) and Richard (born 1849) appear in the 1850 Louisville census with Cornelia but disappear thereafter. He also lost two infants by Frances in Alton. Mary (born 1863) died at six days; her brother William (born 1864) lived for about forty-eight hours. Two others died before reaching adulthood. Cornelia's namesake (born 1852) died in 1860 in Cleveland after an unspecified accident. Conway's namesake (born 1865 to Frances) drowned in a swimming accident in Alton when he was fifteen years old.

Two sons by Cornelia reached maturity. Joseph (born 1850), who served as a page to the Arkansas General Assembly when his father was a legislator, told the Freedman's Bureau in May 1871 that he was a teacher working for "the public." He married Hattie Wilkerson of Madison County, Illinois, on 28 November 1878 and headed to Chicago, where he worked as a waiter, porter, calciminer, and laborer. They had no children. In the late 1880s, he briefly went to Los Angeles, apparently for health reasons. He died at his sister's home in Chicago of chronic interstitial nephritis 15 April 1889. Famous heart surgeon Dr. Daniel Hale Williams signed the death certificate; Reverend Jordan Chavis conducted the funeral. Joseph was forty years old.

Edward was born 12 February 1857 in Cleveland. In 1880 he was working as a bell tender (bellhop) at the Plankinton House in Milwaukee. Throughout the 1880s, he worked as a railroad porter in Chicago. He married Ida Hart, 12 July 1888, in Milwaukee and thereafter worked on the railroad from Jersey City, New Jersey. By 1896, however, he was back in Chicago and without Ida. He stayed until 1900 and then removed to Denver. There he married a woman named Belle; a daughter, Marguerite, was born 18

October 1901. Edward continued to work on the railroad until about 1915 and then became a waiter at a restaurant.

According to his death certificate, Edward committed suicide on 11 July 1917 by stabbing himself with a knife in his left breast. He was sixty years old. The certificate itself contains several errors and omissions. Both of his parents' names are misreported, as is the name of the informant, listed as Josephine M. Barbour. Edward had a sister named Josephine, but her last name in 1917 was Alsup. He is buried in Riverside Cemetery in Denver. Belle lived in their home on Williams Street in Denver until at least the early 1930s. Marguerite married twice. Her first marriage, to World War I veteran Clifford Alsop—no known relation to Aunt Josie's husband—ended in divorce after only a year or so. Alsop died in Stockton, California, in September 1964. Her second husband, Leonard Sandridge, died a couple of months later in Seattle. Marguerite, who had no children, died in 1974.

Catherine (Kate), Conway and Cornelia's oldest child, was born in 1845. In May 1870, she married a barber, John H. Diggs, in Chicago. A son, Gordon, was born in 1873. The 1880 census lists Kate as a dressmaker; her mother and a sister were part of the household. The Diggses enjoyed some standing in the community, even hosting the editor of the *Western Appeal* (St. Paul, Minnesota) at a luncheon in their home in April 1888. Kate's health, however, was fragile. She died of tuberculosis ("phthisis pulmonalis") 13 January 1890 after a lengthy battle. John Diggs was registered to vote in Chicago in 1892 but thereafter disappears. Gordon cannot be found after the 1880 census.[1]

Two of Barbour's daughters by Frances, Lillie and Minnie, married professional men and had public careers of their own. Lillian (Lillie) was born 10 January 1871 in Alton, just as her father was taking his seat in the Arkansas legislature. She taught briefly after graduating high school and then married Charles B. Jones, a schoolteacher and political operative—including service as mayor—in Brooklyn, Illinois, "America's First Black Town." After Jones died in 1925, Lillie married Julius Marshall, an undertaker who had trained with the Officer family. The Marshalls operated an ambulance service and mortuary on Missouri Avenue in East St. Louis for many years. He died 7 June 1951. Lillie, who was childless, lived another six years. She was residing in the Mary Frances Nursing Home in Robertson, Missouri, when she died 22 September 1957 of "senile cycosis." She was eighty-six.[2]

Lillie's sister Minnie was born in 1869 and graduated from Alton High School in 1886. A good student, her name appeared in the Alton's *Telegraph*'s "Scholarship Report," which listed those students whose academic average exceeded 90 percent. After graduation, she taught briefly in Quincy,

Illinois, but left the profession to marry William L. Brown, son of African Methodist Episcopal (AME) bishop John Mifflin Brown, on 3 December 1887 in Alton. A daughter, Beulah, was born in Washington, DC, in August 1888, but the marriage did not last, and Minnie retook her maiden name when she returned to Alton. She taught there in the 1891–92 school year and in Cairo, Illinois, the following academic year.

In 1893, Minnie went to Chicago and became corporation clerk in the Cook County Recorder of Deeds Office, a position she held for about ten years. She also took up her pen, contributing articles on race affairs in Chicago to several black publications. Her 14 September 1901 column in the *Colored American* (Washington, DC) criticizing Booker T. Washington's second annual convention of the National Negro Business League in Chicago as just a bunch of men blowing their own horns prompted a direct rebuttal in the same publication from Washington's friend Fannie Barrier Williams.[3]

In October 1904, she married Dr. George W. Mosby, of Columbus, Ohio, where the couple made their home for the next five decades. Around 1915, Minnie served as secretary of the Columbus chapter of the National Association for the Advancement of Colored People and was involved in the fight to keep *Birth of a Nation* from being shown in the state of Ohio. In the early 1920s, daughter Beulah, who also taught for the Alton School District for several years, married Wade H. Franklin in Columbus. She died at the Mosby home on 8 August 1926 of heart disease at age thirty-eight. Her body was returned to Alton and is buried in the family plot in Upper Alton Cemetery.[4]

Minnie, a member of the Twentieth Century Club of the St. Paul AME Church, died of a heart attack on the morning of Sunday, 1 July 1951. George, who remarried shortly after Minnie's death, died 27 November 1952. Described in the newspaper as the "dean of colored physicians in Columbus," the Howard-educated doctor was also state treasurer for the Knights of Pythias and active in the Sigma Pi Phi Boulé. The couple is buried side by side in Columbus's Green Lawn Cemetery.[5]

Child	Born	Mother	Married	Children	Died	Buried
Catherine (Kate) dressmaker	1845 Louisville	Cornelia	John H. Diggs (barber) in May 1870	Gordon b. 1873 Ohio Not found after 1880	Chicago 13 Jan. 1890 tuberculosis	Oak Woods Cemetery, Chicago
Lucien	1846 Louisville	Cornelia	Appears only in 1850 census; death, burial unknown			
Thomas C. boatman	1848 Louisville	Frances	Virginia Wright b. 1 Sept. 1850 d. 28 Jan. 1928	Thomas Conway Rankin b. 15 Apr. 1874 d. 8 Jan. 1942	Unknown Died or disappeared before 1874	Unknown
Richard	1849 Louisville	Cornelia	Appears only in 1850 census; death, burial unknown			
Joseph R. page, teacher, waiter, porter	1850 Louisville	Cornelia	Hattie Wilkerson on 28 Nov. 1878	None	Chicago 15 Apr. 1889 chronic interstitial nephritis	Oak Woods Cemetery, Chicago
Josephine (Josie) dressmaker, businesswoman	1854 Louisville	Cornelia	John Curry on 12 Mar. 1883 Samuel Alsup in 1894	None	Unknown	Unknown
Cornelia	1852 Cleveland	Cornelia			Cleveland 31 May 1860 accident	Erie Street Cemetery, Cleveland

Table continued

Child	Born	Mother	Married	Children	Died	Buried
Edward Charles railroad porter	12 Feb. 1857 Cleveland	Cornelia	Ida Hart on 12 July 1888 Belle ? in 1900	Marguerite b. 18 Oct. 1901 d. 4 Oct. 1974 (childless)	Denver 11 July 1917 suicide	Riverside Cemetery, Denver
Frances E. (Fannie) schoolteacher	2 Aug. 1860 Alton	Frances	Never married; no children		Alton 8 May 1922 diabetes	Upper Alton Cemetery, Alton
Julia M. schoolteacher, matron	1861 Alton	Frances	Never married; no children		Chicago 12 July 1895 tuberculosis	Upper Alton Cemetery, Alton
Mary E.	9 Feb. 1863 Alton	Frances	Died at 6 days old		15 Feb. 1863	Upper Alton Cemetery, Alton
William C.	1 Feb. 1864 Alton	Frances	Died at 1.5 days old		3 Feb. 1864	Upper Alton Cemetery, Alton
Conway L.	1865 Alton	Frances			Alton May 1880 drowned	Upper Alton Cemetery, Alton

Table continued

Child	Born	Mother	Married	Children	Died	Buried
Minnie teacher, clerk, writer, activist	1869 Alton	Frances	William Brown on 3 Dec. 1887 (d. Mar. 1936) Dr. George W. Mosby in Oct. 1904 (d. 27 Nov. 1952)	Beulah Brown b. Aug. 1888 in Washington, DC m. Wade H. Franklin in Columbus in early 1920s d. 8 Aug. 1928 (childless)	Columbus 1 July 1951 heart attack	Green Lawn Cemetery, Columbus
Lillian G. teacher, business-woman	10 Jan. 1871 Alton	Frances	Charles B. Jones (d. 1925) Julius L. Marshall	None	Robertson, MO 22 Sept. 1957 "senile cycosis"	Upper Alton Cemetery, Alton
Florence A. schoolteacher	June 1875 Arkansas	Frances	Never married; no children		St. Louis 6 July 1918 after surgery	Upper Alton Cemetery, Alton

Notes

INTRODUCTION

1. *Alton Telegraph*, 5 May 1871; Alton Deed Book 2, 868, 27 May 1871, Alton Deed Records.

2. Stuart M. Blumin, *The Emergence of the Middle Class: Social Experience in the American City, 1760–1900* (Cambridge: Cambridge University Press, 1989); Melanie Archer and Judith R. Blau, "Class Formation in Nineteenth-Century America: The Case of the Middle Class," *Annual Review of Sociology* 19 (1993): 17–41; Richard L. Bushman, *The Refinement of America: Persons, Houses, Cities* (New York: Vintage Books, 1993); Karen Halttunen, *Confidence Men and Painted Women: A Study of Middle-Class Culture in America, 1830–1870* (New Haven, CT: Yale University Press, 1982).

3. William Julius Wilson, *The Declining Significance of Race: Blacks and Changing American Institutions* (Chicago: University of Chicago Press, 1978), 144, 150; Karyn R. Lacy, *Blue-Chip Black: Race, Class, and Status in the New Black Middle Class* (Berkeley: University of California Press, 2007), 23–29.

4. Bushman, *Refinement*, 434; Erica L. Ball, *To Live an Antislavery Life: Personal Politics and the Antebellum Black Middle Class* (Athens: University of Georgia Press, 2012).

5. Robert Brent Toplin, "Between Black and White: Attitudes toward Southern Mulattoes, 1830–1861," *Journal of Southern History* 45, no. 2 (May 1979): 188–93, 197–200; Ira Berlin, *Slaves without Masters: The Free Negro in the Antebellum South* (New York: New Press, 1974), 178–79.

6. Berlin, *Slaves without Masters*, 218, 221–22, 229, 234, 240–42; Richard Wade, *Slavery in the Cities: The South, 1820–1860* (London: Oxford University Press, 1964), 248; Leonard Curry, *The Free Black in Urban America, 1800–1850: The Shadow of the Dream* (Chicago: University of Chicago Press, 1981), 16.

7. Gunnar Myrdal, *An American Dilemma: The Negro Problem in Modern Democracy* (1944; repr., New Brunswick, NJ: Transaction, 1996), 2; Berlin, *Slaves without Masters*, 218; Bushman, *Refinement*, 437.

8. Cyprian Clamorgan, *The Colored Aristocracy of St. Louis*, ed. Julie Winch (Columbia: University of Missouri Press, 1999), 8–9; William H. Gibson, *History of the United Brothers of Friendship and Sisters of the Mysterious Ten, in Two Parts* (1897; repr., Freeport, NY: Books for Libraries Press, 1971), pt. 2, 32; William Simmons, *Men of Mark* (1887; repr., Chicago: Johnson, 1970); Leon Litwack and August Meier, eds., *Black Leaders of the Nineteenth Century* (Urbana: University of Illinois Press, 1988), xii.

1. LEXINGTON AND LOUISVILLE

1. James M. Duff, Duff's Funeral Notices Scrap Book, 1806–1887, image 20, Kentucky Digital Library, University of Kentucky, http//:kdl.kyvl.org; Fayette County Clerk, Land Records, K26A, K6, K7; *Kentucky Reporter*, 9 February 1831, Lexington Public Library.

2. John D. Wright Jr., *Lexington: Heart of the Bluegrass* (Lexington, KY: Lexington–Fayette County Historic Preservation Commission, 1982), 75–76; Catherine Clinton, *Mrs. Lincoln: A Life* (New York: Harper Perennial, 2009), 20–21; William H. Townsend, *Lincoln and the Bluegrass: Slavery and Civil War in Kentucky* (Lexington: University of Kentucky Press, 1955), 72–73.

3. Townsend, *Lincoln and the Bluegrass*, 53–57.

4. Townsend, *Lincoln and the Bluegrass*, 79–80; Wright, *Lexington*, 73–74.

5. George Washington Ranck, *History of Lexington, Kentucky: Its Early Annals and Recent Progress, Including Biographical Sketches and Personal Reminiscences of the Pioneer Settlers, Notices of Prominent Citizens, Etc., Etc.* (Cincinnati: Robert Clarke, 1872), 325–27; *Kentucky Reporter*, 22 August 1833, Lexington Public Library; Wright, *Lexington*, 42; Clinton, *Mrs. Lincoln*, 26.

6. Joy Carden, *Music in Lexington before 1840* (Lexington, KY: Lexington–Fayette County Historic Preservation Commission, 1980), 20–22; Julius Bolivar Mac Cabe, *Directory of the City of Lexington and County of Fayette for 1838 & 1839* (Lexington, KY: J. C. Noble, 1838), 63, Fayette County, Kentucky Genealogy and History, www.rootsweb.ancestry.com/~kyfayett/fayette.htm; Lester S. Levy Sheet Music Collection, Johns Hopkins University.

7. U.S. Census, 1860, Slave Schedule, Louisville, Kentucky, ancestry.com. Cornelia's age in the 1830 census is misreported as demonstrated by later censuses.

8. *Kentucky Reporter*, 9 September 1822, Lexington Public Library; *Kentucky Gazette*, 28 April 1826, 6 October 1826, 13 January 1825, Kentucky Digital Library.

9. Charles D. Lowery, *James Barbour, a Jeffersonian Republican* (Tuscaloosa: University of Alabama Press, 1984), 2–12.

10. U.S. Census, 1820, Virginia and Kentucky; U.S. Census, 1830, Virginia and Kentucky, ancestry.com.

11. A newspaper article cited him as an example of successful former slaves. *Morning (Little Rock) Republican*, 3 March 1871; *Arkansas Gazette*, 8 July 1876; personal communication with Charles D. Lowery; *Charlestown (WV) Daily Gazette*, 14 April 1897.

12. Lowery, *James Barbour*, 40–41, 205; James Barbour Papers, microfilm, Special Collections Department, University of Virginia Library.

13. James Barbour Papers, University of Virginia Library.

14. James Barbour Papers, University of Virginia Library.

15. Townsend, *Lincoln and the Bluegrass*, 75–79; Clinton, *Mrs. Lincoln*, 23–25; Willard B. Gatewood, "Sunnyside: The Evolution of an Arkansas Plantation," in *Shadows over Sunnyside: An Arkansas Plantation in Transition, 1830–1945*, ed. Jeannie W. Whayne (Fayetteville: University of Arkansas Press, 1993), 4–6; Thomas J. Goliber, "Cuyahoga Blacks: A Social and Demographic Study, 1850–1880" (MA thesis, Kent State University, 1972), 97.

16. Jefferson County Court Order Book 18, 10 October 1842, 524; 10 January 1843, 554, Filson Historical Society; Jefferson County Court Minute Book, 8 October 1844, n.p., Filson Historical Society.

17. U.S. Census, 1850, Louisville, Kentucky, ancestry.com.

18. See Karolyn Smardz Frost, *I've Got a Home in Glory Land: A Lost Tale of the Underground Railroad* (New York: Farrar, Straus and Giroux, 2007), 133–35, for Quarrier's role in the 1833 escape from Louisville of Thornton and Ruthie Blackburn. Frost argues against suggestions that Quarrier assisted the runaways. U.S. Census, 1850, Louisville, Kentucky, ancestry.com; California Department of Insurance, Slave Era Insurance Registry, www.insurance.ca.gov/01-consumers/150-other-prog/10-seir/; John B. Jegli, *Louisville City Directory, 1845–1846*, 46; and Jegli, *Louisville Directory for 1848*, page number illegible, Filson Historical Society; Louisville Tax Records, 1850 Louisville Tax List, Filson Historical Society.

19. Marion B. Lucas, *A History of Blacks in Kentucky*, vol. 1 of *From Slavery to Segregation* (Frankfort: Kentucky Historical Society, 1992), 115; Gibson, *United Brothers*, pt. 2, 30; John W. Blassingame, ed., *Slave Testimony: Two Centuries of Letters, Speeches, Interviews and Autobiographies* (Baton Rouge: Louisiana State University Press, 1977), 385–86.

20. George H. Yater, *Two Hundred Years at the Falls of the Ohio: A History of Louisville and Jefferson County*, 2nd ed. (Louisville: Filson Club, 1987), 46–60; Isabel McLennan McMeekin, *Louisville: The Gateway City* (New York: Julian Messner, 1946), 91–93; John F. Kleber, ed., *The Encyclopedia of Louisville* (Lexington: University Press of Kentucky, 2001), 714.

21. McMeekin, *Gateway City*, 90–91, 104–7; Faith K. Pizor, "The Great Steam Duck," *Technology and Culture* 9, no. 1 (January 1968): 86–89; Ben Casseday, *The History of Louisville from Its Earliest Settlement till the Year 1852* (1852; repr., Louisville: G. R. Clark, 1970), 246.

22. Robert Gudmestad, *Steamboats and the Rise of the Cotton Kingdom* (Baton Rouge: Louisiana State University Press, 2011); Thomas C. Buchanan, *Black Life on the Mississippi: Slaves, Free Blacks, and the Western Steamboat World* (Chapel Hill: University of North Carolina Press, 2004); Gibson, *United Brothers*, pt. 2, 25–30, 32.

23. Gibson, *United Brothers*, pt. 2, 32.

24. Louis C. Hunter, *Steamboats on the Western Rivers: An Economic and Technological History* (Cambridge, MA: Harvard University Press, 1949), 443; Thomas C. Buchanan, "Rascals on the Antebellum Mississippi: African American Steamboat Workers and the St. Louis Hanging of 1841," *Journal of Social History* 34, no. 4 (2001): n28; Buchanan, *Black Life*, 64, 66, 181–84. In "Rascals," Buchanan estimated that the river trades employed two thousand free blacks and two thousand slaves.

25. Mark Twain, *Life on the Mississippi* (New York: Signet Classics, 2001), 82.

26. Steven Hahn, *A Nation under Our Feet: Black Political Struggles in the Rural South from Slavery to the Great Migration* (Cambridge, MA: Belknap Press of Harvard University Press, 2003); William Wells Brown, "Narrative of William W. Brown: A Fugitive Slave, " in *Four Fugitive Slave Narratives*, ed. Robin W. Winks (Reading, MA: Addison-Wesley, 1969), 22; Thomas C. Buchanan, "Levees of Hope: African American Steamboat Workers, Cities, and Slaves Escapes on the Antebellum Mississippi," *Journal of Urban History* 30, no. 3 (2004): 370; Buchanan, *Black Life*, 102. Hahn notes the importance of antebellum networks of communication for slaves in the rural South. Slaves often sought to be sold to owners who lived near a river. See Walter Johnson, *Soul by Soul: Life inside the Antebellum Slave Market* (Cambridge, MA: Harvard University Press, 1999), 171.

27. J. Blaine Hudson, *Fugitive Slaves and the Underground Railroad in the Kentucky Borderland* (Jefferson, NC: McFarland, 2002), 62, 65–66, 81; William Still, *Still's Underground Rail Road Records* (Philadelphia: William Still, Publisher, 1886); Wilbur H. Siebert, *The Underground Railroad from Slavery to Freedom* (1898; repr., New York: Arno Press and the New York Times, 1968), 70, 151–53; Pamela R. Peters, *The Underground Railroad in Floyd County, Indiana* (Jefferson, NC: McFarland, 2001), 4, 59, 71–74, 82.

28. Buchanan, *Black Life*, 91; Mary Lawrence O'Brien, "Slavery in Louisville during the Antebellum Period, 1820–1860" (MA thesis, University

of Louisville, 1979), 25; McMeekin, *Gateway City*, 121; Hunter, *Steamboats on the Western Rivers*, 445; *Arkansas Gazette*, 11 May 1871.

29. *Louisville Democrat*, 27 January 1848; Jefferson County Circuit Court Records, Old Circuit Court Common Law (Case #39731), Kentucky Department for Libraries and Archives, Frankfort, KY.

30. Lucas, *Blacks in Kentucky*, 108–9.

31. Blassingame, *Slave Testimony*, 385–86.

32. Gibson, *United Brothers*, pt. 2, 5, 40–41. Gibson was later a member of Quinn Chapel.

33. Blassingame, *Slave Testimony*, 385–86, chap. 7.

34. Jegli, *Louisville Directory for 1848*, microfilm, 244, Filson Historical Society; J. T. Hair, *Gazetteer for Madison County* (Evansville, IN: Unigraphic, 1866), 207.

35. Jefferson County Circuit Court Records, case no. missing, Kentucky Department for Libraries and Archives; Minutes of Union Baptist Church, Alton, IL, Church Membership List, privately held by Charlotte Johnson, reviewed March 2007; Benedict Joseph Webb, *The Centenary of Catholicity in Kentucky* (Louisville: C. A. Rogers, 1884), 515.

36. Lowell H. Harrison and James C. Klotter, *A New History of Kentucky* (Lexington: University Press of Kentucky, 1997), 168–69, 174–75.

37. Harold D. Tallant, *Evil Necessity: Slavery and Political Culture in Antebellum Kentucky* (Lexington: University Press of Kentucky, 2003), 29.

38. Harrison and Klotter, *New History*, 177–78.

39. *National Era* (Washington, DC), 5 October 1848; *North Star* (Rochester, NY), 6 October 1848. Isaac L. Hyatt's name is often reported at "J. L." Hyatt, a misprint.

40. Hanford Dozier Stafford, "Slavery in a Border City: Louisville, 1790–1860," (PhD diss., University of Kentucky, 1982), chaps. 6 and 7; *National Era* (Washington, DC), 15 March 1849; *North Star* (Rochester, NY), 25 May 1849.

41. *National Era* (Washington, DC), 11 October 1849; Tallant, *Evil Necessity*, 147–50, 156.

42. Tallant, *Evil Necessity*, 156–58; O'Brien, "Slavery in Louisville," 92.

43. O'Brien, "Slavery in Louisville," 49, 67–68.

44. Gibson, *United Brothers*, pt. 2, 24.

45. Gibson, *United Brothers*, pt. 2, 34.

2. CLEVELAND

1. Patrick Rael, *Black Identity & Black Protest in the Antebellum North* (Chapel Hill: University of North Carolina Press, 2002), 5; R. J. Young,

Antebellum Black Activists: Race, Gender, and Self (New York: Garland, 1996), 182, 185–86.

2. Floyd J. Miller, *The Search for a Black Nationality: Black Emigration and Colonization, 1787–1863* (Urbana: University of Illinois Press, 1975). See also Frank A. Rollin, *Life and Public Services of Martin R. Delany* (1883; repr., New York: Arno Press and the New York Times, 1969); Victor Ullman, *Martin R. Delany: The Beginnings of Black Nationalism* (Boston: Beacon, 1971); and Robert S. Levine, *Martin Delany, Frederick Douglass, and the Politics of Representative Identity* (Chapel Hill: University of North Carolina Press, 1997), among others.

3. Miller, *Search for a Black Nationality*, 117, 120. Other historians downplay Delany's nationalism. Cf. Tommie Shelby, "Two Conceptions of Black Nationalism: Martin Delany on the Meaning of Political Solidarity," *Political Theory* 31, no. 5 (October 2003): 664–92; Tunde Adeleke, *Without Regard to Race: The Other Martin Robison Delany* (Jackson: University Press of Mississippi, 2003).

4. Miller, *Search for a Black Nationality*, 128.

5. For a discussion of the rivalry between the two men, see Levine, *Martin Delany, Frederick Douglass*; Robert S. Levine, ed., *Martin R. Delany: A Documentary Reader* (Chapel Hill: University of North Carolina Press, 2003), 240, 243; *Frederick Douglass' Paper* (Rochester, NY), 19 August 1853, 18 November 1853, 2 December 1853.

6. Howard Holman Bell, *A Survey of the Negro Convention Movement, 1830–1861* (New York: Arno Press and the New York Times, 1969), 1, 5.

7. Bell, *Negro Convention Movement*, 133, 136–37. For the view that colonization efforts never appealed to many blacks, see Louis R. Mehlinger, "The Attitude of the Free Negro toward African Colonization," *Journal of Negro History* 1, no. 3 (June 1916): 276–301; Elizabeth Rauh Bethel, *The Roots of African-American Identity, Memory and History in Antebellum Free Communities* (New York: St. Martin's, 1997), 141.

8. Miller, *Search for a Black Nationality*, 137n4.

9. Miller, *Search for a Black Nationality*, 144–45.

10. *Proceedings of the National Emigration Convention of Colored People; Held at Cleveland, Ohio, on Thursday, Friday, and Saturday, the 24th, 25th and 26th of August, 1854* (Pittsburgh: A. A. Anderson, 1854), 10, 12–13.

11. The secretaries of the convention corrected the error in his last name but not his first. Perhaps Barbour had a southern accent that gave his name three syllables instead of two. Gibson also recorded Barbour's first name as "Conoway."

12. Levine, *Martin R. Delany: Documentary Reader*, 291–96, 325. Shadd married Thomas Cary in January 1856. Jane Rhodes, *Mary Ann Shadd Cary:*

The Black Press and Protest in the Nineteenth Century (Bloomington: Indiana University Press, 1998), 112, 117, 120; Miller, *Search for a Black Nationality*, 165–66; C. Peter Ripley, ed., *The Black Abolitionist Papers*, vol. 2, *Canada, 1830–1865* (Chapel Hill: University of North Carolina Press, 1986), 341n1; "Abstract of the Minutes of the Cleveland National Convention," *Provincial Freeman* (Chatham, Canada West), 25 November 1856.

13. *New York Times*, 29 August 1854, 8 August 1855.

14. Cuyahoga County Probate Court Records, Cuyahoga County Recorder of Deeds Book 156, 411; Book 91, 308; U.S. Census, 1860, Cleveland, Ohio, ancestry.com.

15. Stephen Middleton, *The Black Laws: Race and the Legal Process in Early Ohio* (Athens: Ohio University Press, 2005), 13; Frank U. Quillen, *The Color Line in Ohio: A History of Race Prejudice in a Typical Northern State* (1913; repr., New York: Negro Universities Press, 1969), 15; Bessie House-Soremekun, *Confronting the Odds: African American Entrepreneurship in Cleveland, Ohio* (Kent, OH: Kent State University Press, 2002); Joe William Trotter Jr., *River Jordan: African American Urban Life in the Ohio Valley* (Lexington: University Press of Kentucky, 1998); "An Ordinance for the Government of the Territory of the United States Northwest of the River Ohio," House Document No. 398, in *Documents Illustrative of the Formation of the Union of the American States*, selected, arranged, and indexed by Charles C. Tansil (Washington, DC: Government Printing Office, 1927). Article 3 provided for fair treatment of Native Americans. See also Eugene H. Berwanger, *The Frontier against Slavery: Western Anti-Negro Prejudice and the Slavery Extension Controversy* (Urbana: University of Illinois Press, 1967); V. Jacque Voegeli, *Free but Not Equal: The Midwest and the Negro during the Civil War* (Chicago: University of Chicago Press, 1967); Leon F. Litwack, *North of Slavery: The Negro in the Free States, 1790–1860* (Chicago: University of Chicago Press, 1961).

16. Quillen, *Color Line*, 17, 21–22; Middleton, *Black Laws*, 41, 47; James H. Rodabaugh, "The Negro in Ohio," *Journal of Negro History* 31, no. 1 (January 1946): 14–16.

17. Middleton, *Black Laws*, 62–63; Quillen, *Color Line*, 32.

18. Middleton, *Black Laws*, 137; Quillen, *Color Line*, 37.

19. Middleton, *Black Laws*, chap. 7 and p. 209.

20. Kenneth L. Kusmer, *A Ghetto Takes Shape: Black Cleveland, 1870–1930* (Urbana: University of Illinois Press, 1976), 6.

21. Kusmer, *Ghetto Takes Shape*, 29; House-Soremekun, *Confronting the Odds*, 15–16.

22. Goliber, "Cuyahoga Blacks," 19, 23, 97, 107; U.S. Census, 1860, Cleveland, Ohio, ancestry.com.

23. Goliber, "Cuyahoga Blacks," 65, 95, 102.

24. Quillen, *Color Line*, 154. John Malvin, *North into Freedom: The Autobiography of John Malvin, Free Negro, 1795–1880*, ed. and introduced by Allan Peskin (Kent, OH: Kent State University Press, 1988), 14–15.

25. Bell, *Negro Convention Movement*, 298; House-Soremekun, *Confronting the Odds*, 14; U.S. Census, 1860, Cleveland, Ohio, ancestry.com; Ripley, *Abolitionist Papers*, 394–95n7.

26. *Proceedings of the National Emigration Convention*, 8; Malvin, *North into Freedom*, 20.

27. Malvin, *North into Freedom*, 43; Middleton, *Black Laws*, 70–71; Nikki Taylor, "Reconsidering the 'Forced' Exodus of 1829: Free Black Emigration from Cincinnati, Ohio to Wilberforce, Canada," *Journal of African American History* 87, no. 3 (Summer 2002): 283–302. Taylor says that only some African Americans fled because of the violence and that many more left in an organized fashion, not as victims, but in an act of self-determination.

28. Malvin, *North into Freedom*, 49.

29. Curry, *Free Black in Urban America*, and Berlin, *Slaves without Masters*, argue this was typical. Malvin, *North into Freedom*, 50–51, 55–57.

30. *Alton Weekly Courier*, 6 January 1859; U.S. Census, 1860, Alton, Illinois, ancestry.com.

31. Michael Grossberg, *Governing the Hearth: Law and the Family in Nineteenth-Century America* (Chapel Hill: University of North Carolina Press, 1985), 121; *Alton Telegraph*, 29 November 1853; *Chicago Tribune*, 31 August 1857; *Alton Telegraph*, 3 May 1854; *Chicago Tribune*, 12 August 1857, 12 October 1853; *Baltimore Sun*, 24 January 1840.

32. *Salem (IL) Weekly Advocate*, 25 May 1854; *Ottawa (IL) Free Trader*, 12 March 1847; Christopher Robert Reed, *Black Chicago's First Century*, vol. 1, *1833–1900* (Columbia: University of Missouri Press, 2005), 287–88.

33. Beverly Schwartzberg, "'Lots of Them Did That': Desertion, Bigamy, and Marital Fluidity in Late-Nineteenth-Century America," *Journal of Social History* 37, no. 3 (Spring 2004): 576, 579. Men did not start wearing wedding rings until the twentieth century. See Vicki Howard, "A 'Real Man's Ring': Gender and the Invention of Tradition," *Journal of Social History* 36, no. 4 (Summer 2003): 837.

34. Schwartzberg, "Lots of Them," 581–82, 588; *Ottawa (IL) Free Trader*, 29 December 1848; *Alton Telegraph*, 16 April 1853.

35. *Loomis & Talbott's Cleveland City Directory for 1861* (Cleveland: Herald Office Print, 1861), 15; *Baker's Cleveland Directory, 1864–65* (Cleveland: Fairbanks, Benedict, 1864), 131; *Cleveland Leader City Directory for 1866–67* (Cleveland: Cleveland Leader, 1866), 43; *Cleveland Leader Annual City*

Directory for 1867–68 (Cleveland: Cleveland Leader, 1867), 103; *Wiggins & Weaver's Directory of the City of Cleveland and Adjoining Towns for 1870–71* (Cleveland: Wiggins & Weaver, 1870), 73; *W.S. Robison & Co.'s Cleveland Directory, 1871–72* (Cleveland: W. S. Robison, 1871), 65.

36. Cuyahoga County Probate Court Records, Ohio Probate Files, 1813–1932, Docket E, Case no. 448; *Cleveland Leader City Directory for 1869* (Cleveland: Cleveland Leader, 1869), 9; *W.S. Robison's Cleveland Directory 1873* (Cleveland: W. S. Robison, 1873), 45.

37. U.S. Census, 1860, Cleveland, Ohio; U.S. Census, 1870, Cleveland, Ohio, ancestry.com.

38. Schwartzberg, "Lots of Them," 574, 585.

39. James Oliver Horton, *Free People of Color: Inside the African American Community* (Washington, DC: Smithsonian Institution, 1993), 98–120.

40. Maria W. Stewart, "Throw Off Your Fearfulness and Come Forth," in *Black Women in White America: A Documentary History*, ed. Gerda Lerner (New York: Vintage Books, 1992), 527; Shirley J. Carlson, "Black Ideals of Womanhood in the Late Victorian Era," *Journal of Negro History* 77, no. 2 (Spring 1992): 61–73.

3. ALTON

1. Military historian Edwin C. Bearrs emphasized the importance of Harper's Ferry as a rallying cry for southerners in *Fields of Honor: Pivotal Battles of the Civil War* (Washington, DC: National Geographic, 2006), 19. He made the same argument in Ken Burns's film *The Civil War.*

2. Paul Simon, *Freedom's Champion, Elijah Lovejoy* (Carbondale: Southern Illinois University Press, 1994), 134–35, 141–42.

3. Calculated from Elsie M. Wasser, transcriber, *1845 Census of Madison County, Illinois* (Edwardsville, IL: privately published, 1985). The total population of the county was 18,013.

4. Calculated from Maxine E. Wormer, transcriber, *Madison County, Illinois, 1850 Census* (Thomson, IL: Heritage House, 1976); calculated from Joyce Upton, transcriber, *Madison County, Illinois, 1860 Census* (Utica, KY: McDowell Publications, 1986); calculated from the 1865 State of Illinois Census, Madison County Census, microfilm, Illinois State Archives, Springfield, IL; U.S. Census, 1870, Madison County, Illinois, ancestry.com; U.S. Census, 1880, Madison County, Illinois, ancestry.com.

5. U.S. Census, 1850, Alton, Illinois, ancestry.com; *National Era* (Washington, DC), 10 February 1853. The editor of the paper promised to continue Howard's subscription regardless of his ability to pay. *Frederick Douglass' Paper* (Rochester, NY) picked up the story on 24 February 1853;

W. T. Norton, *Centennial History of Madison County, Illinois, and Its People, 1812–1912* (Chicago: Lewis, 1912), 213–17.

6. Stephen Middleton, *The Black Laws in the Old Northwest: A Documentary History* (Westport CT: Greenwood, 1993), 271, 333.

7. Film and transcriptions of "Negro Book Register of Papers Belonging to Free Persons of Colour" are held by the Madison County Historical Museum and Archives, Edwardsville, IL; Edward A. Miller Jr., *The Black Civil War Soldiers of Illinois: The Story of the Twenty-Ninth U.S. Colored Infantry* (Columbia: University of South Carolina Press, 1988), 7. See also Voegeli, *Free but Not Equal*, 1–11; Middleton, *Old Northwest*, 274, 298–99.

8. *Proceedings of the State Convention of Colored Citizens of the State of Illinois, Held in the City of Alton, November 13th, 14th, and 15th, 1856* (Chicago: Hays and Thompson, 1856), 3–4; Committee on Black Pioneers, *20th Century African American Leaders in Alton* (Alton, IL: Alton Museum of History and Art, 2001), 13; Jeffrey B. Allen, *Alton, Illinois: A Graphic Sketch of a Picturesque and Busy City* (St. Louis: James Allan Reid, 1912), 84.

9. Middleton, *Old Northwest*, 274; *Proceedings of the State Convention*, 3–4, 17–18; Charles A. Gliozzo, "John Jones and the Black Convention Movement, 1848–1856," *Journal of Black Studies* 3, no. 2 (1972): 227–36; Levine, *Martin R. Delany: A Documentary Reader*, 243.

10. *Proceedings of the State Convention*, 8. The vote was seven to excise the language and seven to retain, with four abstaining or absent. With no majority for excision tallied, the language remained in the document.

11. Miller, *Soldiers of Illinois*, 8.

12. *Alton Weekly Courier*, 17 June 1858, 3 February 1859.

13. Norton, *Centennial History*, 236; *Alton Weekly Courier*, 21 October 1858. A week earlier the Republican *Courier*, on 14 October 1858, suggested that Douglas was wasting his time in Madison County.

14. Norton, *Centennial History*, 236–37; *Alton Weekly Courier*, 21 October 1858.

15. The 1860 results were Lincoln, 3,161; Douglas, 3,100; Bell, 178; Breckenridge, 21. In 1864, Lincoln received 3,156 votes; McClellan, 3,287. Norton, *Centennial History*, 229. These figures are confirmed in John Moses, *Illinois, Historical and Statistical* (Chicago: Fergus, 1892), 1209. The *Alton Telegraph*'s 1864 election results had 3,180 for Lincoln and 3,301 for McClellan and reported Lincoln losing to McClellan in Alton 614 to 724. The paper said Lincoln won by a single vote in Upper Alton, 246 to 245. *Alton Telegraph*, 17 November 1865; Richard Steckel, "Migration and Political Conflict: Precincts in the Midwest on the Eve of the Civil War," *Journal of Interdisciplinary History* 28, no. 4 (Spring 1998): 583–603. Although Steckel

does not address Madison County specifically, his evidence suggests that southern migrants had an adverse effect on Lincoln's vote totals in other Illinois counties. James Simeone, *Democracy and Slavery in Frontier America: The Bottomland Republic* (DeKalb: Northern Illinois University Press, 2000). Early Illinoisans were very concerned with the rights of "white folks," a sentiment that persisted.

16. *Alton Telegraph*, 27 April 1861.

17. *Alton Telegraph*, 15 November 1861, 6 June 1862, 18 October 1861.

18. William Wells Brown, *The Negro in the American Rebellion: His Heroism and Fidelity* (1867, repr., Athens: Ohio University Press, 2003, with an introduction and annotations by John David Smith), 82–83. Brown incorrectly gave the date as 27 May 1862, when in fact it was a year earlier.

19. *Alton Telegraph*, 31 May 1861.

20. Brown, *Negro in the American Rebellion*, 83–84; also in Miller, *Soldiers of Illinois*, 8; *Alton Telegraph*, 4 December 1863.

21. James M. McPherson, *The Negro's Civil War: How American Blacks Felt and Acted during the War for Union* (New York: Ballantine Books, 1991), 22 passim. Noah Andre Trudeau, *Like Men of War: Black Troops in the Civil War, 1862–1865* (Boston: Little, Brown, 1998), 7–13, 18; Miller, *Soldiers of Illinois*, 5–6, 32. For the constitutional and political debates regarding confiscation of slaves, see Silvana Siddali, *From Property to Person: Slavery and the Confiscation Acts, 1861–1862* (Baton Rouge: Louisiana State University Press, 2005). See also Dorothy L. Drinkard, *Illinois Freedom Fighters: A Civil War Saga of the 29th Infantry, United States Colored Troops* (Needham, MA: Simon & Schuster Custom, 1998), 9–17. Drinkard's small volume details the history of the unit but does not address the soldiers as individuals.

22. Civil War Records of the 29th U.S. Colored Regiment, Microfilm Project #47, reel 28, Records Management Division, Illinois State Archives, Springfield, IL. I decided against inserting "[*sic*]" after his many spelling errors.

23. Buchanan, *Black Life on the Mississippi*, 69.

24. Conway Barbour to Richard Yates, Chronicling Illinois (collection), Abraham Lincoln Presidential Library and Museum, http://alplm-cdi.com /chroniclingillinois/items/show/8509. Again, I decided against flagging every spelling error.

25. Norton, *Centennial History*, 391–92. Hunter discusses the brief boom for steamboats at the outset of the Civil War and the decline thereafter as railroad supplanted the river traffic. Hunter, *Steamboats on the Western Rivers*, 561.

26. *Gazetteer of Madison County* (Alton, IL), 96–97; John Sibley Butler, *Entrepreneurship and Self-Help among Black Americans: A Reconsideration*

of Race and Economics (Albany: State University of New York Press, 2005), 47; Edwin Adams Davis and William Ransom Hogan, *The Barber of Natchez* (Baton Rouge: Louisiana State University Press, 1954), 39–40; probate records for Henry Blair, box 29, tray 90, Illinois State Archives, Illinois Regional Archives Depository System, Southern Illinois University, Carbondale, IL.

27. *Alton Telegraph*, 30 October 1863; Madison County Deed Book 77, 160; *Alton Telegraph*, 10 February 1865.

28. Madison County Deed Book 80, 421–22. A quitclaim is a deed or legal paper in which a person releases or relinquishes a claim on a property to another person. Alton Deed Book 1, 232.

29. 1865 State of Illinois Census, Madison County.

30. *Alton Telegraph*, 10 February 1865.

31. U.S. Census, 1860, Springfield, Illinois, ancestry.com.

32. *Alton Telegraph*, 3 April 1861.

33. *Alton Telegraph*, 12 May 1865; Cuyahoga County Recorder of Deeds, Book 133, 529–30, Cuyahoga County Probate Court Records; Alton Deed Book 1, 71.

34. Louis S. Gerteis, *Civil War St. Louis* (Lawrence: University of Kansas Press, 2001), 201; Norton, *Centennial History*, 478.

35. *Alton Telegraph*, 9 March 1866; 6 April 1866.

36. Gary R. Kremer, *James Milton Turner and the Promise of America: The Public Life of a Post–Civil War Black Leader* (Columbia: University of Missouri Press, 1991), 22–23; *Alton Telegraph*, 12 January 1866, 2 February 1866.

37. *Alton Telegraph*, 6 April 1866.

38. Madison County Deed Book 86, 364–65. Barbour retained possession of the items; provisions were made for default and sale. Alton Deed Record Book 3, 622; Book 1, 756.

39. Madison County Deed Book 89, 343–44.

40. *Alton Telegraph*, 20 September 1867.

41. Madison County Deed Book 89, 527–28; Book 94, 55–56.

42. *Alton Telegraph*, 10 January 1868, 28 February 1868.

43. *Alton Telegraph*, 27 March 1868, 15 May 1868.

44. Hunter, *Steamboats on the Western Rivers*, 613n16.

45. Charlotte Stetson, *Alton, Illinois: A Pictorial History* (St. Louis: G. Bradley, 1986), 133; *Holland's Alton City Directory for 1868–1869* (Chicago: Western Publishing, 1868), 32, 47, 53, 67, 76, 92, 93, 101, 106, 111; Cuyahoga County Deed Records, Book 156, 162; Book 156, 411; Book 177, 579–80; Book 186, 221–24.

46. *Alton Telegraph*, 13 March 1868, 18 December 1868.

47. *Alton Telegraph*, 28 August 1868; *Morning Republican* (Little Rock), 24 July 1869.

48. Minutes of the Union Baptist Church, Alton, IL, Church Membership List, privately held by Charlotte Johnson, reviewed March 2007; *Alton Telegraph*, 17 May 1867.

49. *Morning Republican* (Little Rock), 24 July 1869; 25 November 1869; 15 December 1869.

4. LITTLE ROCK

1. Eric Foner, *Freedom's Lawmakers: A Directory of Black Officeholders during Reconstruction* (New York: Oxford University Press, 1993), xi–xxxi; Stephen Middleton, ed., *Black Congressmen during Reconstruction: A Documentary Sourcebook* (Westport, CT: Praeger, 2002); Eric Foner, *Reconstruction: America's Unfinished Revolution, 1863–1877* (New York: Harper & Row, 1988).

2. Calculated from U.S. Census, 1870, ancestry.com. Foner, *Freedom's Lawmakers*, xiii–xiv; Alrutheus A. Taylor, *The Negro in the Reconstruction of Virginia* (Washington, DC: Association for the Study of Negro Life and History, 1926), 3; Alrutheus A. Taylor, *The Negro in South Carolina during the Reconstruction* (Washington, DC: Association for the Study of Negro Life and History, 1924), 310–11; William A. Dunning, *Reconstruction, Political and Economic, 1865–1877* (New York: Harper & Brothers, 1907). The basics of the Dunning-school interpretation are discussed in Foner, *Reconstruction: America's Unfinished Revolution*, xix–xx. See also Eric Foner, "Reconstruction Revisited," *Reviews in American History* 10, no. 4 (December 1982): 82–100; and Alrutheus A. Taylor, "Historians of the Reconstruction," *Journal of Negro History* 23, no. 1 (January 1938): 16–34. Daniel Savage Gray points out that black commentators saw earlier and more accurately than whites the nature of Reconstruction. Gray, "Bibliographical Essay: Black Views on Reconstruction," *Journal of Negro History* 58, no. 1 (January 1973): 73–85.

3. Taylor, *Virginia*, 285; Taylor, *South Carolina*, 157; W. E. B. DuBois, *Black Reconstruction* (Philadelphia: Albert Saifer, 1935) 417, 442, 507, 577; John Hosmer and Joseph Fineman, "Black Congressmen in Reconstruction Historiography," *Phylon* 39, no. 2 (Summer 1978): 97–107; Euline W. Brock, "Thomas W. Cardozo: Fallible Black Reconstruction Leader," *Journal of Southern History* 47, no. 2 (May 1981): 184; Elizabeth Balanoff, "Negro Legislators in the North Carolina General Assembly, July 1868–February 1872," in *The Politics of Freedom: African Americans and the Political Process during Reconstruction*, ed. Donald G. Nieman (New York: Garland, 1994);

Allen W. Trelease, "Republican Reconstruction in North Carolina: A Roll-Call Analysis of the State House of Representatives, 1868–1870," *Journal of Southern History* 42, no. 3 (August 1976): 319–44; Joseph M. St. Hilaire, "The Negro Delegates in the Arkansas Constitutional Convention of 1868: A Group Profile," *Arkansas Historical Quarterly* 32, no. 1 (Spring 1974): 38–69; Richard L. Hume, "The Arkansas Constitutional Convention of 1868: A Case Study in the Politics of Reconstruction," *Journal of Southern History* 39, no. 2 (May 1973): 183–206; Walter J. Fraser Jr., "Black Reconstructionists in Tennessee," in *Politics of Freedom*, ed. Nieman.

4. Armstead Robinson, "Beyond the Realm of Social Consensus: New Meanings of Reconstruction for American History," *Journal of American History* 68, no. 2 (September 1981): 292; David C. Rankin, "The Origins of Black Leadership in New Orleans during Reconstruction," *Journal of Southern History* 40, no. 3 (August 1974): 417–40; Thomas Holt, *Black over White: Negro Political Leadership in South Carolina during Reconstruction* (Urbana: University of Illinois Press, 1977); Edmund L. Drago, *Black Politicians and Reconstruction in Georgia: A Splendid Failure* (Baton Rouge: Louisiana State University Press, 1982); Foner, *Reconstruction: America's Unfinished Revolution*, 377. This view is also apparent in Heather Cox Richardson, *The Death of Reconstruction: Race, Labor, and Politics in the Post–Civil War North, 1865–1901* (Cambridge, MA: Harvard University Press, 2001); and Julie Saville, *The Work of Reconstruction: From Slave to Wage Laborer in South Carolina, 1860–1870* (Cambridge: Cambridge University Press, 1996).

5. Michael W. Fitzgerald, "Reconstruction Politics and the Politics of Reconstruction," in *Reconstructions: New Perspectives on the Postbellum United States*, ed. Thomas J. Brown (New York: Oxford University Press, 2006), 91–116.

6. Foner, *Freedom's Lawmakers*, 13, 21, 108, 127.

7. Foner, *Freedom's Lawmakers*, 4–5, 13–14, 105–6, 162–63.

8. Foner, *Freedom's Lawmakers*, xxviii, 175–76.

9. Carl H. Moneyhon, *The Impact of the Civil War and Reconstruction on Arkansas: Persistence in the Midst of Ruin* (Fayetteville: University of Arkansas Press, 2002), 13–34, 176; Thomas A. DeBlack, *With Fire and Sword: Arkansas, 1861–1874* (Fayetteville: University of Arkansas Press, 2003), 1–5. See also S. Charles Bolton, *Arkansas, 1800–1860: Remote and Restless* (Fayetteville: University of Arkansas Press, 1998), 125–44, on the relationship between cotton and slavery.

10. Moneyhon, *Impact of the Civil War*, 33.

11. Moneyhon, *Impact of the Civil War*, 128, 140. During the war, Confederate troops in Arkansas massacred black Union troops as well as unarmed

fugitive slaves at Poison Springs and Mark's Mill. African American troops responded in kind by slaughtering wounded Confederates at Jenkins' Ferry. See Gregory J. W. Urwin, "'We Cannot Treat Negroes . . . as Prisoners of War': Racial Atrocities and Reprisals in Civil War Arkansas," in *Civil War Arkansas: Beyond Battles and Leaders*, ed. Anne J. Bailey and Daniel E. Sutherland (Fayetteville: University of Arkansas Press, 2000), 213–29.

12. DeBlack, *Fire and Sword*, 105.

13. Moneyhon, *Impact of the Civil War*, 190–91, 195–96. For the traditional view of disfranchisement as vindictive radicalism, see Eugene G. Feistman, "Radical Disfranchisement in Arkansas, 1867–1868," *Arkansas Historical Quarterly* 12, no. 2 (Summer 1953): 126–68.

14. Moneyhon, *Impact of the Civil War*, 198–201, 203; DeBlack, *Fire and Sword*, 149.

15. Moneyhon, *Impact of the Civil War*, 242.

16. Moneyhon, *Impact of the Civil War*, 245; Cal Ledbetter Jr., "The Constitution of 1868: Conqueror's Constitution or Constitutional Continuity?" *Arkansas Historical Quarterly* 44, no. 1 (Spring 1985): 16–41. Hume stressed the solidarity of the eight black delegates to the convention in support of its "radical agenda." Hume, "Arkansas Constitutional Convention," 201.

17. William H. Burnside, *The Honorable Powell Clayton* (Conway: University of Central Arkansas Press, 1991), 25–27; Orval Truman Driggs Jr., "The Issues of the Powell Clayton Regime, 1868–1871," *Arkansas Historical Quarterly* 8, no. 1 (Spring 1949): 9–14.

18. Moneyhon, *Impact of the Civil War*, 250–51.

19. DeBlack, *Fire and Sword*, 185, 191–99. Four more counties were added later.

20. Moneyhon, *Impact of the Civil War*, 252–53.

21. Burnside, *Powell Clayton*, 39.

22. Letters of Powell Clayton, 4 January 1870 to 24 September 1870, microfilm, Arkansas State Archives, 119.

23. Delazon Smith Papers, collection 26, box 2, folders 8 and 9, Oregon Historical Society Research Library.

24. Letters of Powell Clayton, 266, Arkansas State Archives; Burnside, *Powell Clayton*, 39–40.

25. Letters of Powell Clayton, 644, Arkansas State Archives.

26. U.S. Census, 1870, Lewisville, Arkansas; U.S. Census, 1870, Alton, Illinois, ancestry.com; Letters of Powell Clayton, 496, Arkansas State Archives.

27. Bobby L. Lovett, "African Americans, Civil War, and Aftermath in Arkansas," *Arkansas Historical Quarterly* 54, no. 3 (Autumn 1995): 333–34; Billy D. Higgins, "Act 151 of 1859," Encyclopedia of Arkansas History and

Culture, Butler Center for Arkansas Studies at the Central Arkansas Library System, last updated 3 May 2012, http://encyclopediaofarkansas.net.

28. Moneyhon, *Impact of the Civil War*, 66–67, 71.

29. Moneyhon, *Impact of the Civil War*, 211–12.

30. Asst. Adjt. General to Bureau Refugees, Freedmen and Abandoned Lands for Arkansas and Indian Territory, 24 November 1866, roll 52, National Archives Microfilm Publication M979, Freedmen's Bureau Online, Bureau of Refugees, Freemen and Abandoned Lands, 1865–1869, http://freedmensbureau.com/arkansas/arkreport.htm.

31. Daniel F. Littlefield Jr. and Patricia Washington McGraw, "The Arkansas Freeman, 1869–1870—Birth of the Black Press in Arkansas," *Phylon* 40, no. 1 (1979): 75–85.

32. Lovett, *Aftermath in Arkansas*, 336.

33. Papers of Powell Clayton, 644, Arkansas State Archives.

34. *Morning Republican* (Little Rock), 12 August 1870, 22 October 1870.

35. *Morning Republican* (Little Rock), 17 November 1870; Driggs, "Issues of Powell Clayton Regime," 12.

36. John Henderson and C. Albertson, *Little Rock City Directory, 1871* (Little Rock: Price & Barton, 1871). Neither Conway nor Joseph was listed in the directory since it was published after the legislative session was over and both had left the city. U.S. Census, 1870, Little Rock, Arkansas, ancestry.com.

37. George S. Taft, *Compilation of Senate Election Cases from 1789 to 1885* (Washington, DC: Government Printing Office, 1885), 418.

38. See Blake Wintory, "William Hines Furbush: African American Carpetbagger, Republican, Fusionist, and Democrat," *Arkansas Historical Quarterly* 63, no. 2 (Summer 2004): 107–61; Christopher Waldrep, *Roots of Disorder: Race and Criminal Justice in the American South, 1817–1880* (Urbana: University of Illinois Press, 1998); Michael W. Fitzgerald, *Urban Emancipation: Popular Politics in Reconstruction Mobile, 1860–1890* (Baton Rouge: Louisiana State University Press, 2002).

39. Moneyhon, *Impact of the Civil War*, 257.

40. Cortez A. M. Ewing, "Arkansas Reconstruction Impeachments," *Arkansas Historical Quarterly* 13, no. 2 (Summer 1954): 137; Cortez A. M. Ewing, "Florida Reconstruction Impeachments," *Florida Historical Quarterly* 30, no. 4 (1958): 299–318. Foner said Reed had a "tacit agreement with Conservatives to run the state on the principles of white supremacy and economic development," in *Reconstruction: America's Unfinished Revolution*, 330–31; Cortez A. M. Ewing, "Two Reconstruction Impeachments," *North Carolina Historical Review* 15, no. 3 (July 1938): 204–30;

Foner, *Reconstruction: America's Unfinished Revolution*, 440–41. Ewing argued that the removal was correct because Holden used martial law for political purposes. More recent historians disagree. Cf. Edgar E. Folk and Bynum Shaw, *W. W. Holden: A Political Biography* (Winston-Salem, NC: John F. Blair, 1982); Nicholas Lemann, *Redemption: The Last Battle of the Civil War* (New York: Farrar, Straus and Giroux, 2006), 160–64.

41. *Journal of the House of Representatives, State of Arkansas, Session of 1871* (Little Rock: Price & McClure, 1871), 73–74.

42. *Journal of the House*, 104–10.

43. *Journal of the House*, 226–30, 237–38, 250–54.

44. U.S. Freedmen's Bank Records, 1865–1874, South Carolina, 1866, 262, record 5, ancestry.com.

45. *Journal of the House*, 307.

46. Wintory, "William Hines Furbish," 107, 124; Mifflin W. Gibbs, *Shadow and Light: An Autobiography* (1902; repr., New York: Arno Press and the New York Times, 1968); Tom Dillard, "'Golden Prospects and Fraternal Amenities': Mifflin W. Gibbs's Arkansas Years," *Arkansas Historical Quarterly* 25, no. 4 (Winter 1976): 307–33.

47. *Journal of the House*, 317.

48. *Journal of the House*, 332, 369–71, 376–77.

49. *Journal of the House*, 381.

50. *Arkansas Gazette*, 18 January 1872; Taft, *Compilation*, 418.

51. *Journal of the House*, 394–97.

52. *Journal of the House*, 398, 408–9.

53. *Journal of the House*, 409.

54. *Journal of the House*, 394.

55. *Journal of the House*, 425, 511–14.

56. *Journal of the House*, 517–19.

57. *Journal of the House*, 538–40, 548, 581–85, 638–40.

58. Burnside, *Powell Clayton*, 46.

59. *Journal of the House*, 715–16; *Arkansas Gazette*, 5 January 1872.

60. *Journal of the House*, 1005–6.

61. DeBlack, *Fire and Sword*, 213; *Journal of the House*, 882, 947.

62. *Morning Republican* (Little Rock), 3 March 187; Michael Cobb and Jeffery Jenkins have asserted that black U.S. congressmen during Reconstruction were significantly more representative of black interests than white Republicans representing similar constituencies, although they do not assert the same would be found at the state level. Michael D. Cobb and Jeffery A. Jenkins, "Race and the Representation of Blacks' Interests during Reconstruction," *Political Research Quarterly* 54, no. 1 (March 2001):

181–204. Their argument is at odds with another writer who challenged the idea that majority-minority congressional districts necessarily maximized the representation of black interests. Cf. Carol M. Swain, *Black Faces, Black Interests: The Representation of African Americans in Congress* (Cambridge, MA: Harvard University Press, 1993).

63. Merline Pitre, *Through Many Dangers, Toils & Snares: Black Leadership in Texas, 1870–1890* (Austin: Eakin, 1992), 168–216.

64. *Journal of the House*, 622.

5. LAKE VILLAGE, ARKANSAS

1. Moneyhon, *Impact of the Civil War*, 17; Willard B. Gatewood, "Sunnyside: The Evolution of an Arkansas Plantation, 1840–1945," in *Shadows over Sunnyside*, ed. Whayne, 4–6.

2. Thomas DeBlack, "A Garden in the Wilderness: The Johnsons and the Making of Lakeport Plantation, 1831–1876" (PhD diss., University of Arkansas, 1995), 266; *New National Era* (Washington, DC), 10 March 1870; Gatewood, "Sunnyside," 7–8.

3. *Morning Republican* (Little Rock), 21 March 1870; *Arkansas Gazette*, 21 March 1871, quoting the *Cincinnati Commercial*. Only one member of the Arkansas House was deemed acceptable by the *Commercial*, but the paper's derisive comment about steamboat deckhands suggests it was not referring to Barbour.

4. Calculated form the U.S. Census, 1870, ancestry.com.

5. U.S. Census, 1870, McConnell Township, Chicot County, Arkansas, ancestry.com.

6. Desmond Walls Allen, ed., *Arkansas State Donation and Swamp Lands: Arkansas, Chicot, and Desha Counties, 1855–2001* (Conway: Arkansas Research, 2003), 5–7.

7. Allen, *Arkansas State Donation*, 104–5, 167, 170; Chicot County Deed Record Book O, 1871–1872, microfilm, roll 48, 322–29, Arkansas State Archives.

8. *Arkansas Gazette*, 20 January 1872. The article referred to appointed probate judges, but all Republican-appointed officials benefited in counties where blacks were in the majority. *Arkansas Gazette*, 2 May 1871; *Atlanta Constitution*, 5 May 1871.

9. Taft, *Compilation*, 416.

10. *Arkansas Gazette*, 9 May 1871.

11. Fay Hempstead, *A Pictorial History of Arkansas from Earliest Times to the Year 1890* (St. Louis: N. D. Thompson, 1890), 913.

12. *Arkansas Gazette*, 9 May 1871.

13. *Arkansas Gazette*, 11 May 1871.

14. Glenn C. Altschuler and Stuart M. Blumin, *Rude Republic: Americans and Their Politics in the Nineteenth Century* (Princeton, NJ: Princeton University Press, 2000); Mark E. Neely Jr., *The Boundaries of American Political Culture in the Civil War Era* (Chapel Hill: University of North Carolina Press, 2005), 5, 7.

15. Chicot County Deed Record Book O, 391. During Barbour's tenure in the state legislature, the House considered a bill to authorize Thomas D. Martin of Jefferson County to practice law, but the bill did not pass.

16. Chicot County Deed Record Book O, 331–32; Bushman, *Refinement*, 231; Chicot County Deed Record Book O, 330 notation.

17. U.S. Census, 1870, Chicot County, Arkansas; DeBlack, *Fire and Sword*, 264–65.

18. *Arkansas Gazette*, 17 May 1872, 13 July 1872. The bonds were finally put on the market after a third vote in the spring of 1872. Resentment about these bond issues was evident decades later. Commenting on the "salubrious" nature of Chicot County, Leona Brasher wrote around 1915 that, despite its natural virtues, the county was

> handicapped by bonds issued in the early '70s. . . . This bond indebtedness was instigated by men in charge during the reconstruction period when one of their tools was County Judge J. W. Mason, a Negro. Bonds were issued in the amount of $300,000.00 to build railroads running from Little Rock to New Orleans. These bonds were sold for cash in New York. The money was used by "Carpet Bag" graft and not one cent went into any railroad. We are now paying a 5-mill tax each year toward this debt, have on hand about $55,000.00 in local banks, carrying a small interest. When this $240,000.00 is paid, our county will be free of debt once more and greater improvements in every way will mark this era.

Leona Brasher, "An Historical Manuscript of Chicot County," in *A Tribute to Chicot County, Arkansas*, ed. Sheila Farrell Brannon (Arkansas: privately published, 2000), 37, http://www.sabrahome.net/text/TributeToChicot County.pdf.

19. *Arkansas Gazette*, 31 December 1871; J. Clay Smith Jr., *Emancipation: The Making of the Black Lawyer, 1844–1944* (Philadelphia: University of Pennsylvania Press, 1993), 322.

20. *Arkansas Gazette*, 31 December 1871; DeBlack, *Fire and Sword*, 267.

21. *Ohio Democrat* (New Philadelphia, OH), 29 December 1871; *Arkansas Gazette*, 28 December 1871, 3 January 1872, 1.

22. *Arkansas Gazette*, 22 December 1871; DeBlack, *Fire and Sword*, 268.

23. Foner, *Reconstruction: America's Unfinished Revolution*, 436–37; Lemann, *Redemption*, 3–29, 142–43. The Colfax massacre led to the *United States v. Cruikshank* decision in 1875, in which the U.S. Supreme Court said enforcement of civil rights for blacks was a state, not federal, matter.

24. *Arkansas Gazette*, 27 December 1871; *Atlanta Constitution*, 24 December 1871; *Bangor (ME) Daily Whig and Courier*, 27 December 1871; *New York Herald*, 27 December 1871; *Arkansas Gazette*, 31 December 1871.

25. DeBlack, *Fire and Sword*, 269; see *Lake Shore Sentinel* (Luna, AR) for the years 1876–77.

26. Smith, *Emancipation*, 323; 1865 State of Illinois Census, Madison County.

27. Thomas S. Staples, *Reconstruction in Arkansas, 1862–1874* (New York: Columbia University, 1923), 373–74; James H. Atkinson, "The Arkansas Gubernatorial Campaign and Election of 1872," *Arkansas Historical Quarterly* 1, no. 4 (December 1942): 307n2, 308n3; Earl F. Woodward, "The Brooks and Baxter War in Arkansas, 1872–1874," *Arkansas Historical Quarterly* 30, no. 4 (Winter 1971): 317n6. Baxter, a slaveholder who opposed secession, was once charged with treason by the Confederacy, but he escaped jail and then accepted a commission in the Union Army.

28. *Arkansas Gazette*, 30 April 1872.

29. *Arkansas Gazette*, 18 August 1872.

30. *Arkansas Gazette*, 20 August 1872, 21 August 1872, 23 August 1872.

31. *Arkansas Gazette*, 22 August 1872.

32. *Arkansas Gazette*, 24 August 1872.

33. *Arkansas Gazette*, 19 November 1872.

34. Moneyhon, *Impact of the Civil War*, 260; DeBlack, *Fire and Sword*, 218–19; Woodward, "Brooks and Baxter War," 320–22; Foner, *Reconstruction: America's Unfinished Revolution*, 528.

35. Woodward, "Brooks and Baxter War," 326.

36. DeBlack, *Fire and Sword*, 219–23; Moneyhon, *Impact of the Civil War*, 261; Woodward, "Brooks and Baxter War," 327–34.

37. Woodward, "Brooks and Baxter War," 327, 331.

38. Foner, *Reconstruction: America's Unfinished Revolution*, 528.

39. Moneyhon, *Impact of the Civil War*, 262; C. Vann Woodward, *The Strange Career of Jim Crow* (New York: Oxford University Press, 2002). See also John William Graves, "Jim Crow in Arkansas: A Reconsideration of Urban Race Relations in the Post-Reconstruction South," *Journal of Southern History* 55, no. 3 (August 1989): 421–48.

40. *Arkansas Gazette*, 8 January 1873.

41. Chicot County Tax Records, McConnell Township, Lists of Persons and Personal Property Assessed for Taxation, microfilm roll 71, 81; Foner, *Reconstruction: America's Unfinished Revolution*, 512, 532.

42. Chicot County Tax Records, McConnell Township, Lists of Persons and Personal Property Assessed for Taxation, microfilm roll 71, 81; Chicot County Deed Record Book P, 576–77, 718–21; Book Q, 605.

43. Chicot County Deed Record Book S, 979–81; Book T, 8–9, 160–61.

44. Louis Wiltz, *The Great Mississippi Flood of 1874: Its Extent, Duration and Effects. A Circular from Mayor Wiltz, of New Orleans, to the Mayors of American Cities and Towns, and to the Philanthropic throughout the Republic, in Behalf of Seventy Thousand Sufferers in Louisiana Alone* (New Orleans: Picayune Steam Book and Job Print, 1874), 1–8; DeBlack, *Fire and Sword*, 209.

45. Chicot County Will Record Book C, 234–35; Chicot County Court Record Book D, 702, 779.

CONCLUSION

1. *Arkansas Gazette*, 8 July 1876; *Cincinnati Daily Star*, 26 July 1876.

2. *Reports of Cases at Law and in Equity Argued and Determined in the Supreme Court of the State of Arkansas*, vol. 35 (Little Rock: Arkansas Union Printing and Publishing, 1881), *Ford v. Tallman*, 548–55.

3. The Columbian Exposition ran from 1 May to 30 October 1893.

4. *Reports of the Cases Decided in the Appellate Courts of the State of Illinois*, vol. 58 (Chicago: Callaghan, 1895), 421–27. Julia's mother, Frances, and sister Minnie were listed as residents of the same Chicago address at which Julia died. The following year, Frances and four of her other daughters were living at the same address, 441 S. Robey. Conway's first wife, Cornelia, and her remaining children were also in Chicago in the mid-1890s, on Armour Avenue, making it plausible, perhaps likely, that Conway's two families were in contact.

5. *Western Appeal* (St. Paul, MN), 26 May 1888, 30 June 1888, 14 July 1888.

6. For a re-creation of the incident, see Elizabeth Dale's excellent article "'Social Equality Does Not Exist among Themselves, nor among Us': *Baylies vs. Curry* and Civil Rights in Chicago, 1888," *American Historical Review* 102, no. 2 (April 1997): 311–39. The drawing of Josie Curry on the front page of the *Chicago Tribune* of 16 March 1888 is a rare depiction of anyone in the Barbour family.

7. Dale, "Social Equality," 320.

8. See Shirley J. Portwood, "The Alton School Case and African American Community Consciousness, 1897–1908," *Illinois Historical Journal* 91,

no. 1 (Spring 1998): 2–20. The case is formally known as *The People of the State of Illinois, ex rel., Scott Bibb v. The Mayor and Common Council of the City of Alton.*

9. Quoted in Portwood, "Alton School Case," 13.

10. *Alton Telegraph*, 8 July 1918, 8 May 1922.

11. U.S. Census, 1860, Alton, Madison County, Illinois; 1870, Alton, Madison County, Illinois; *U.S. Social Security Applications and Claims Index*, ancestry.com.

12. *Weekly Town Talk* (Alexandria, LA), 5 May 1900; *Times-Picayune* (New Orleans), 15 June 1898; U.S. Census, 1920, Alton, Madison County, Illinois, ancestry.com.

APPENDIX: THE OTHER CHILDREN

1. *Western Appeal* (St. Paul, MN), 14 April 1888.

2. Sundiata Keita Cha-Jua, *America's First Black Town: Brooklyn, Illinois, 1830–1915* (Urbana: University of Illinois Press, 2000).

3. *Colored American* (Washington, DC) 14 September 1901, 28 September 1901.

4. "Sixth Annual Report," *Crisis* 11, no. 5 (March 1916): 257. The *Crisis* was the magazine of the National Association for the Advancement of Colored People from 1910 to 1923. See also Herbert Aptheker, ed., *A Documentary History of the Negro People in the United States*, vol. 3, *1910–1932* (New York: Carol, 1993), 149–50.

5. *Columbus (OH) Dispatch*, 28 November 1952.

Bibliography

PRIMARY SOURCES

Census Records
U.S. Census, 1850. www.ancestry.com.
U.S. Census, 1860. www.ancestry.com.
U.S. Census, 1870. www.ancestry.com.
1845 Census of Madison County, Illinois. Transcribed by Elsie Wasser. Edwardsville, IL: privately published, 1985.
1865 State of Illinois Census, Madison County Census. Transcribed by Joyce Upton. Illinois State Archives, Springfield, IL. Microfilm.

Newspapers
Alton Telegraph (Alton, IL).
Alton Weekly Courier (Alton, IL).
Arkansas Gazette (Little Rock, AR).
Atlanta Constitution (Atlanta, GA).
Baltimore Sun (Baltimore, MD).
Bangor Daily Whig and Courier (Bangor, ME).
Charlestown Daily Gazette (Charlestown, WV).
Chicago Tribune (Chicago, IL).
Colored American (Washington, DC).
Frederick Douglass' Paper (Rochester, NY).
Kentucky Gazette (Lexington, KY).
Kentucky Reporter (Lexington, KY).
Lake Shore Sentinel (Luna, AR).
Louisville Democrat (Louisville, KY).
Morning Republican (Little Rock, AR).
National Era (Washington, DC).
New National Era (Washington, DC).

New York Herald (New York, NY).
New York Times (New York, NY).
North Star (Rochester, NY).
Ohio Democrat (New Philadelphia, OH).
Ottawa Free Trader (Ottawa, IL).
Provincial Freeman (Chatham, Canada West).
Salem Weekly Advocate (Salem, IL).
Western Appeal (St. Paul, MN).

City and County Records

Alton City Directories. Hayner Library, Alton, IL.
Alton Deed Records. Madison County Recorder of Deeds, Edwardsville, IL.
Barbour Collection of Connecticut Vital Records. ancestry.com.
Chicot County Deed Records, Arkansas State Archives.
Chicot County Tax Records, Arkansas State Archives.
Cleveland City Directories, Cuyahoga County Archives.
Cleveland Death Index, Cuyahoga County Archives.
Cuyahoga County Probate Court Records.
Department of Public Health, City of Chicago, Undertaker's Report of Death.
Fayette County Clerk, Land Records, Lexington, KY.
Hair, J. T. *Gazetteer of Madison County, 1866.* Evansville, IN: Unigraphic, 1866.
Henderson, John, and C. Albertson. *Little Rock City Directory, 1871.* Little Rock: Price & Barton, 1871.
Jefferson County Circuit Court Records. Kentucky Department for Libraries and Archives, Frankfort, KY.
Jefferson County Court Minute Books. Filson Historical Society.
Jefferson County Court Order Books. Filson Historical Society.
Jefferson County Estate Settlement Books. Filson Historical Society.
Jefferson County Marriage Certificates. Filson Historical Society.
Jegli, John B. Louisville City Directories. Filson Historical Society.
Louisville Tax Records. Filson Historical Society.
Mac Cabe, Julius Bolivar. *Directory of the City of Lexington and County of Fayette for 1838 & 1839.* Lexington, KY: J. C. Noble, 1838.
Madison County Deed Records. Madison County Recorder of Deeds, Edwardsville, IL.
Minutes of Union Baptist Church, Alton, IL. Privately held by Charlotte Johnson.

"Negro Book Register of Papers Belonging to Free Persons of Color."
Madison County Historical Museum and Archives, Edwardsville, IL.
Upper Alton Cemetery Records. Upper Alton Cemetery, Alton, IL.

Pamphlets and Proceedings

Bill of Fare of the Louisville & New Orleans Packet Eclipse, E. T. Sturgeon,
Commander. Louisville: J. F. Brennan, 1855. Missouri Historical Society.

Journal of the House of Representatives, State of Arkansas, Session of 1871.
Little Rock: Price & McClure, 1871.

Proceedings of the National Emigration Convention of Colored People; Held
at Cleveland, Ohio, on Thursday, Friday, and Saturday, the 24th, 25th
and 26th of August, 1854. Pittsburgh: A. A. Anderson, 1854.

Proceedings of the State Convention of Colored Citizens of the State of Illinois,
Held in the City of Alton, November 13th, 14th, and 15th, 1856. Chicago:
Hays and Thompson, 1856.

Wiltz, Louis. *The Great Mississippi Flood of 1874. Its Extent, Duration and*
Effects. A Circular from Mayor Wiltz, of New Orleans, to the Mayors of
American Cities and Towns, and to the Philanthropic throughout the
Republic, in Behalf of Seventy Thousand Sufferers in Louisiana Alone.
New Orleans: Picayune Steam Book and Job Print, 1874.

Other

Bureau of Refugees. Freeman and Abandoned Lands, 1865–1869. National
Archives.

Civil War Records of the 29th U.S. Colored Regiment. Microfilm Project
#47, reels 28–30. Records Management Division, Illinois State Archives,
Springfield, IL.

Delazon Smith Papers. Oregon Historical Society Research Library.

Duff, James M. Duff's Funeral Notices Scrap Book, 1806–1887. Kentucky
Digital Library, University of Kentucky. http://kdl.kyvl.org.

Freemen's Bureau Bank Records. ancestry.com.

James Barbour Papers. Special Collections Department, University of Virginia Library.

Lester S. Levy Sheet Music Collection. Johns Hopkins University.

Letters of Powell Clayton. Arkansas State Archives.

"An Ordinance for the Government of the Territory of the United States
Northwest of the River Ohio," House Document No. 398. In *Documents*
Illustrative of the Formation of the Union of the American States, selected,
arranged, and indexed by Charles C. Tansil. Washington, DC: Government Printing Office, 1927.

Slave Era Insurance Registry. California Department of Insurance.

U.S. Department of State, Office of the Historian.

SECONDARY SOURCES

Adeleke, Tunde. *Without Regard to Race: The Other Martin Robison Delany.* Jackson: University of Mississippi Press, 2003.

Allen, Desmond Walls, ed. *Arkansas State Donation and Swamp Lands: Arkansas, Chicot, and Desha Counties, 1855–2001.* Conway: Arkansas Research, 2003.

Allen, Jeffrey B. "'All of Us Are Highly Pleased with the Country': Black and White Kentuckians on Liberian Colonization." *Phylon* 43, no. 2 (1982): 97–109.

———. *Alton, Illinois: A Graphic Sketch of a Picturesque and Busy City.* St. Louis: James Allan Reid, 1912.

Altschuler, Glenn C., and Stuart M. Blumin. *Rude Republic: Americans and Their Politics in the Nineteenth Century.* Princeton, NJ: Princeton University Press, 2000.

Aptheker, Herbert, ed. *A Documentary History of the Negro People in the United States.* Vol. 3, *1910–1932.* New York: Carol, 1993.

Archer, Melanie, and Judith R. Blau. "Class Formation in Nineteenth-Century America: The Case of the Middle Class." *Annual Review of Sociology* 19 (1993): 17–41.

Atkinson, James H. "The Arkansas Gubernatorial Campaign and Election of 1872." *Arkansas Historical Quarterly* 1, no. 4 (December 1942): 307–21.

Bailey, Anne J., and Daniel E. Sutherland, eds. *Civil War Arkansas: Beyond Battles and Leaders.* Fayetteville: University of Arkansas Press, 2000.

Ball, Erika L. *To Live an Antislavery Life: Personal Politics and the Antebellum Black Middle Class.* Athens: University of Georgia Press, 2012.

Barnhart, John D. "Sources of Southern Migration into the Old Northwest." *Mississippi Valley Historical Review* 22, no. 1 (June 1935): 49–62.

Bearrs, Edwin C. *Fields of Honor: Pivotal Battles of the Civil War.* Washington, DC: National Geographic, 2006.

Bell, Howard Holman. "The Negro Emigration Movement, 1849–1854: A Phase of Negro Nationalism." *Phylon* 20, no. 2 (1959): 132–42.

———. *A Survey of the Negro Convention Movement, 1830–1861.* New York: Arno Press and the New York Times, 1969.

Berlin, Ira. *Slaves without Masters: The Free Negro in the Antebellum South.* New York: New Press, 1974.

Berwanger, Eugene H. *The Frontier against Slavery: Western Anti-Negro Prejudice and the Slavery Extension Controversy.* Urbana: University of Illinois Press, 1967.

Bethel, Elizabeth Rauh. *The Roots of African-American Identity: Memory and History in Antebellum Free Communities.* New York: St. Martin's, 1997.

Blassingame, John W., ed. *Slave Testimony: Two Centuries of Letters, Speeches, Interviews, and Autobiographies.* Baton Rouge: Louisiana State University Press, 1977.

Blumin, Stuart M. *The Emergence of the Middle Class: Social Experience in the American City, 1760–1900.* Cambridge: Cambridge University Press, 1989.

Bolton, S. Charles. *Arkansas, 1800–1860: Remote and Restless.* Fayetteville: University of Arkansas Press, 1998.

Brasher, Leona. "An Historical Manuscript of Chicot County." In *A Tribute to Chicot County, Arkansas,* edited by Sheila Farrell Brannon, 34–46. Arkansas: privately published, 2000. http://www.sabrahome.net/text /TributeToChicotCounty.pdf.

Brock, Euline W. "Thomas W. Cardozo: Fallible Black Reconstruction Leader." *Journal of Southern History* 47, no. 2 (May 1981): 183–206.

Brown, Thomas J., ed. *Reconstructions: New Perspectives on the Postbellum United States.* New York: Oxford University Press, 2006.

Brown, William Wells. "Narrative of William W. Brown: A Fugitive Slave." In *Four Fugitive Slave Narratives,* edited by Robin W. Winks. Reading, MA: Addison-Wesley, 1969.

———. *The Negro in the American Rebellion: His Heroism and His Fidelity.* Annotated and introduced by John David Smith. Athens: Ohio University Press, 2003.

Buchanan, Thomas C. *Black Life on the Mississippi: Slaves, Free Blacks, and the Western Steamboat World.* Chapel Hill: University of North Carolina Press, 2004.

———. "Levees of Hope: African American Steamboat Workers, Cities, and Slave Escapes on the Antebellum Mississippi." *Journal of Urban History* 30, no. 3 (March 2003): 360–77.

———. "Rascals on the Antebellum Mississippi: African American Steamboat Workers and the St. Louis Hanging of 1841." *Journal of Social History* 34, no. 4 (2001): 797–816.

Burckin, Alexander. "A 'Spirit of Perseverance': Free African-Americans in Late Antebellum Louisville." *Filson Club History Quarterly* 70, no. 1 (January 1996): 61–81.

Burnside, William H. *The Honorable Powell Clayton.* Conway: University of Central Arkansas Press, 1991.

Bushman, Richard L. *The Refinement of America: Persons, Houses, Cities.* New York: Vintage Books, 1993.

Butler, John Sibley. *Entrepreneurship and Self-Help among Black Americans: A Reconsideration of Race and Economics.* Albany: State University of New York Press, 2005.

Carden, Joy. *Music in Lexington before 1840.* Lexington, KY: Lexington–Fayette County Historic Preservation Commission, 1980.

Carlson, Shirley J. "Black Ideals of Womanhood in the Late Victorian Era." *Journal of Negro History* 77, no. 2 (Spring 1992): 61–73.

———. "Black Migration to Pulaski County, Illinois, 1860–1900." *Illinois Historical Journal* 80, no. 1 (Spring 1987): 37–46.

Casseday, Ben. *The History of Louisville from Its Earliest Settlement till the Year 1852.* Louisville: Hull and Brother, 1852. Reprint, Louisville: G. R. Clark, 1970.

Cha-Jua, Sundiata Keita. *America's First Black Town: Brooklyn, Illinois, 1830–1915.* Urbana: University of Illinois Press, 2000.

Clamorgan, Cyprian. *The Colored Aristocracy of St. Louis.* Edited by Julie Winch. Columbia: University of Missouri Press, 1999.

Clinton, Catherine. *Mrs. Lincoln: A Life.* New York: Harper Perennial, 2009.

Cobb, Michael D., and Jeffery A. Jenkins. "Race and the Representation of Blacks' Interests during Reconstruction." *Political Research Quarterly* 54, no. 1 (March 2001): 181–204.

Committee on Black Pioneers. *20th Century African American Leaders in Alton.* Alton, IL: Alton Museum of History and Art, 2001.

Cornish, Dudley Taylor. *The Sable Arm: Black Troops in the Union Army, 1861–1865.* Lawrence: University Press of Kansas, 1987.

Cramer, Clayton E. *Black Demographic Data, 1790–1860: A Sourcebook.* Westport, CT: Greenwood, 1997.

Curry, Leonard P. *The Free Black in Urban America, 1800–1850: The Shadow of the Dream.* Chicago: University of Chicago Press, 1981.

Dale, Elizabeth. "'Social Equality Does Not Exist among Themselves, nor among Us': *Baylies vs. Curry* and Civil Rights in Chicago, 1888." *American Historical Review* 102, no. 2 (April 1997): 311–39.

Davis, Edwin Adams, and William Ransom Hogan. *The Barber of Natchez.* Baton Rouge: Louisiana State University Press, 1954.

Davis, James E. *Frontier America, 1800–1840: A Comparative Demographic Analysis of the Settlement Process.* Glendale, CA: Arthur H. Clark, 1977.

DeBlack, Thomas A. "A Garden in the Wilderness: The Johnsons and the Making of Lakeport Plantation, 1831–1876." PhD diss., University of Arkansas, 1995.

———. *With Fire and Sword: Arkansas, 1861–1874*. Fayetteville: University of Arkansas Press, 2003.

Dillard, Tom W. "'Golden Prospects and Fraternal Amenities': Mifflin W. Gibbs's Arkansas Years." *Arkansas Historical Quarterly* 25, no. 4 (Winter 1976): 307–33.

———. "To the Back of the Elephant: Racial Conflict in the Arkansas Republican Party." *Arkansas Historical Quarterly* 33, no. 1 (Spring 1974): 3–15.

Drago, Edmund L. *Black Politicians and Reconstruction in Georgia: A Splendid Failure*. Baton Rouge: Louisiana State University Press, 1982.

Driggs, Orval Truman, Jr. "The Issues of the Powell Clayton Regime, 1868–1871." *Arkansas Historical Quarterly* 8, no. 1 (Spring 1949): 1–75.

Drinkard, Dorothy L. *Illinois Freedom Fighters: A Civil War Saga of the 29th Infantry, United States Colored Troops*. Needham, MA: Simon & Schuster Custom, 1998.

DuBois, W. E. B. *Black Reconstruction: An Essay toward a History of the Part Which Black Folk Played in the Attempt to Reconstruct Democracy in America, 1860–1880*. Philadelphia: Albert Saifer, 1935.

Dunning, William A. *Essays on the Civil War and Reconstruction and Related Topics*. New York: Peter Smith, 1931.

———. *Reconstruction, Political and Economic, 1865–1877*. New York: Harper & Brothers, 1907.

Ewing, Cortez A. M. "Arkansas Reconstruction Impeachments." *Arkansas Historical Quarterly* 13, no. 2 (Summer 1954): 137–53.

———. "Florida Reconstruction Impeachments." *Florida Historical Quarterly* 30, no. 4 (1958): 299–318.

———. "Two Reconstruction Impeachments." *North Carolina Historical Review* 15, no. 3 (July 1938): 204–30.

Feistman, Eugene G. "Radical Disfranchisement in Arkansas, 1867–1868." *Arkansas Historical Quarterly* 12, no. 2 (Summer 1953): 125–68.

Fitzgerald, Michael W. *Urban Emancipation: Popular Politics in Reconstruction Mobile, 1860–1890*. Baton Rouge: Louisiana State University Press, 2002.

Folk, Edgar E., and Bynum Shaw. *W. W. Holden: A Political Biography*. Winston-Salem, NC: John F. Blair, 1982.

Foner, Eric. *Freedom's Lawmakers: A Directory of Black Officeholders during Reconstruction*. New York: Oxford University Press, 1993.

———. *Reconstruction: America's Unfinished Revolution, 1863–1877*. New York: Harper & Row, 1988.

———. "Reconstruction Revisited." *Reviews in American History* 10, no. 4 (December 1982): 82–100.

———. *A Short History of Reconstruction*. New York: Harper & Row, 1990.

Frost, Karolyn Smardz. *I've Got a Home in Glory Land: A Tale of the Underground Railroad*. New York: Farrar, Straus and Giroux, 2007.

Genovese, Eugene D. *Roll, Jordan, Roll: The World the Slaves Made*. New York: Vintage Books, 1976.

Gerteis, Louis S. *Civil War St. Louis*. Lawrence: University Press of Kansas, 2001.

Gibbs, Mifflin W. *Shadow and Light: An Autobiography*. New York: Arno Press and the New York Times, 1968.

Gibson, William H. *History of the United Brothers of Friendship and Sisters of the Mysterious Ten, in Two Parts*. Louisville: Bradley & Gilbert, 1897. Reprint, Freeport, NY: Books for Libraries Press, 1971.

Glatthaar, Joseph T. *Forged in Battle: The Civil War Alliance of Black Soldiers and White Officers*. New York: Free Press, 1990.

Gliozzo, Charles A. "John Jones and the Black Convention Movement, 1848–1856." *Journal of Black Studies* 3, no. 2 (December 1972): 227–336.

Goliber, Thomas J. "Cuyahoga Blacks: A Social and Demographic Study, 1850–1880." MA thesis, Kent State University, 1972.

Graves, John William. "Jim Crow in Arkansas: A Reconsideration of Urban Race Relations in the Post-Reconstruction South." *Journal of Southern History* 55, no. 3 (August 1989): 421–48.

Gray, Daniel Savage. "Bibliographical Essay: Black Views on Reconstruction." *Journal of Negro History* 58, no. 1 (January 1973): 73–85.

Grossberg, Michael. *Governing the Hearth: Law and the Family in Nineteenth-Century America*. Chapel Hill: University of North Carolina Press, 1985.

Gudmestad, Robert. *Steamboats and the Rise of the Cotton Kingdom*. Baton Rouge: Louisiana State University Press, 2011.

Hahn, Steven. *A Nation under Our Feet: Black Political Structures in the Rural South from Slavery to the Great Migration*. Cambridge, MA: Belknap Press of Harvard University Press 2003.

Haltunnen, Karen. *Confidence Men and Painted Women: A Study of Middle-Class Culture in America, 1830–1870*. New Haven, CT: Yale University Press, 1982.

Harrison, Lowell H., and James C. Klotter. *A New History of Kentucky*. Lexington: University Press of Kentucky, 1997.

Hempstead, Fay. *A Pictorial History of Arkansas from Earliest Times to the Year 1890.* New York: N. D. Thompson, 1890.

Hine, Darlene Clark, and Earnestine Jenkins, eds. *A Question of Manhood: A Reader in U.S. Black Men's History and Masculinity.* Vol. 1, *"Manhood Rights": The Construction of Black Male History and Manhood, 1750–1870.* Bloomington: Indiana University Press, 1999.

Hine, William C. "Black Politicians in Reconstruction Charleston, South Carolina: A Collective Study." *Journal of Southern History* 49, no. 4 (November 1983): 555–84.

———. *History of Madison County, Illinois. Illustrated, with Biographical Sketches of Many Prominent Men and Pioneers.* Edwardsville, IL: W. R. Brink, 1882.

Holt, Thomas. *Black over White: Negro Political Leadership in South Carolina during Reconstruction.* Urbana: University of Illinois Press, 1977.

Horton, James Oliver. *Free People of Color: Inside the African American Community.* Washington, DC: Smithsonian Institution, 1993.

Horton, James Oliver, and Lois E. Horton. *In Hope of Liberty: Culture, Community and Protest among Northern Free Blacks, 1700–1860.* New York: Oxford University Press, 1997.

Hosmer, John, and Joseph Fineman. "Black Congressmen in Reconstruction Historiography." *Phylon* 39, no. 2 (Summer 1978): 97–107.

House-Soremekun, Bessie. *Confronting the Odds: African American Entrepreneurship in Cleveland, Ohio.* Kent, OH: Kent State University Press, 2002.

Howard, Vicki. "A 'Real Man's Ring': Gender and the Invention of Tradition. *Journal of Social History* 36, no. 4 (Summer 2003): 837–56.

Hudson, J. Blaine. *Fugitive Slaves and the Underground Railroad in the Kentucky Borderland.* Jefferson, NC: McFarland, 2002.

Hume, Richard L. "The Arkansas Constitutional Convention of 1868: A Case Study in the Politics of Reconstruction." *Journal of Southern History* 39, no. 2 (May 1973): 183–206.

Hunter, Louis C. *Steamboats on the Western Rivers: An Economic and Technological History.* Cambridge, MA: Harvard University Press, 1949.

Johnson, Walter. *Soul by Soul: Life inside the Antebellum Slave Market.* Cambridge, MA: Harvard University Press, 1999.

Katzman, David M. *Before the Ghetto: Black Detroit in the Nineteenth Century.* Urbana: University of Illinois Press, 1973.

Kleber, John F., ed. *The Encyclopedia of Louisville.* Lexington: University Press of Kentucky, 2001.

Kremer, Gary R. *James Milton Turner and the Promise of America: The Public Life of a Post–Civil War Black Leader.* Columbia: University of Missouri Press, 1991.

Kunkle, Paul A. "Modifications in Louisiana Negro Legal Status under Louisiana Constitutions, 1812–1957." *Journal of Negro History* 44, no. 1 (January 1959): 1–25.

Kusmer, Kenneth L. *A Ghetto Takes Shape: Black Cleveland, 1870–1930.* Urbana: University of Illinois Press, 1976.

Lacy, Karyn R. *Blue-Chip Black: Race, Class, and Status in the New Black Middle Class.* Berkeley: University of California Press, 2007.

Ledbetter, Calvin R., Jr. "The Constitution of 1868: Conqueror's Constitution or Constitutional Continuity?" *Arkansas Historical Quarterly* 44, no. 1 (Spring 1985): 16–41.

———. "The Long Struggle to End Convict Leasing in Arkansas." *Arkansas Historical Quarterly* 52, no. 1 (Spring 1993): 1–26.

Lemann, Nicholas. *Redemption: The Last Battle of the Civil War.* New York: Farrar, Straus and Giroux, 2006.

Lerner, Gerda, ed. *Black Women in White America: A Documentary History.* New York: Vintage Books, 1992.

Levine, Robert S. *Martin Delany, Frederick Douglass, and the Politics of Representative Identity.* Chapel Hill: University of North Carolina Press, 1997.

———, ed. *Martin R. Delany: A Documentary Reader.* Chapel Hill: University of North Carolina Press, 2003.

Littlefield, Daniel F., and Patricia Washington McGraw. "The Arkansas Freeman, 1869–1870—Birth of the Black Press in Arkansas." *Phylon* 40, no. 1 (1979): 75–85.

Litwack, Leon F. *North of Slavery: The Negro in the Free States, 1790–1860.* Chicago: University of Chicago Press, 1961.

———. *Trouble in Mind: Black Southerners in the Age of Jim Crow.* New York: Vintage Books, 1999.

Litwack, Leon F., and August Meier, eds. *Black Leaders of the Nineteenth Century.* Urbana: University of Illinois Press, 1988.

Lowery, Charles D. *James Barbour, a Jeffersonian Republican.* Tuscaloosa: University of Alabama Press, 1984.

Lovett, Bobby L. "African Americans, Civil War, and Aftermath in Arkansas." *Arkansas Historical Quarterly* 54, no. 3 (Autumn 1995): 304–58.

Lucas, Marion B. *A History of Blacks in Kentucky.* Vol. 1, *From Slavery to Segregation.* Frankfort: Kentucky Historical Society, 1992.

Malvin, John. *North into Freedom: The Autobiography of John Malvin, Free Negro, 1795–1880.* Edited and introduced by Allan Peskin. Kent, OH: Kent State University Press, 1988.

McClelland, Peter D., and Richard J. Zeckhauser. *Demographic Dimensions of the New Republic: American Interregional Migration, Vital Statistics, and Manumissions, 1800–1860.* Cambridge: Cambridge University Press, 1982.

McMeekin, Isabel McLennan. *Louisville: The Gateway City.* New York: Julian Messner, 1946.

McPherson, James M. *The Negro's Civil War: How American Blacks Felt and Acted during the War for Union.* New York: Ballantine Books, 1991.

Mehlinger, Louis R. "The Attitude of the Free Negro toward African Colonization." *Journal of Negro History* 1, no. 3 (June 1916): 276–301.

Meier, August, and Elliot Rudwick. *From Plantation to Ghetto.* New York: Hill and Wang, 1976.

Middleton, Stephen, ed. *Black Congressmen during Reconstruction: A Documentary Sourcebook.* Westport, CT: Praeger, 2002.

———. *The Black Laws in the Old Northwest: A Documentary History.* Westport, CT: Greenwood, 1993.

———. *The Black Laws: Race and the Legal Process in Early Ohio.* Athens: Ohio University Press, 2005.

Miller, Edward A., Jr. *The Black Civil War Soldiers of Illinois: The Story of the Twenty-Ninth U.S. Colored Infantry.* Columbia: University of South Carolina Press, 1988.

Miller, Floyd J. *The Search for a Black Nationality: Black Emigration and Colonization, 1787–1863.* Urbana: University of Illinois Press, 1975.

Moneyhon, Carl. H. *Arkansas and the New South, 1874–1929.* Fayetteville: University of Arkansas Press, 1997.

———. *The Impact of the Civil War and Reconstruction on Arkansas: Persistence in the Midst of Ruin.* Fayetteville: University of Arkansas Press, 2003.

———. "The Impact of the Civil War in Arkansas: The Mississippi River Plantation Counties." *Arkansas Historical Quarterly* 51, no. 2 (Summer 1992): 105–18.

Moses, John. *Illinois, Historical and Statistical.* Chicago: Fergus, 1892.

Myrdal, Gunnar. *An American Dilemma: The Negro Problem in Modern Democracy.* New York: Harper & Brothers, 1944. Reprint, New Brunswick, NJ: Transaction, 1996.

Neely, Mark E., Jr. *The Boundaries of American Political Culture in the Civil War Era.* Chapel Hill: University of North Carolina Press, 2005.

Nieman, Donald G., ed. *The Politics of Freedom: African Americans and the Political Process during Reconstruction*. New York: Garland, 1994.

Norton, W. T. *Centennial History of Madison County, Illinois, and Its People, 1812–1912*. Chicago: Lewis, 1912.

O'Brien, Mary Lawrence. "Slavery in Louisville during the Antebellum Period, 1820–1860." MA thesis, University of Louisville, 1979.

Peters, Pamela R. *The Underground Railroad in Floyd County, Indiana*. Jefferson, NC: McFarland, 2001.

Pitre, Merline. *Through Many Dangers, Toils & Snares: Black Leadership in Texas, 1870–1890*. Austin: Eakin, 1997.

Pizor, Faith K. "The Great Steam Duck." *Technology and Culture* 9, no. 1 (January 1968): 86–89.

Portwood, Shirley J. "The Alton School Case and African American Community Consciousness, 1897–1908." *Illinois Historical Journal* 91, no. 1 (Spring 1998): 2–20.

Quarles, Benjamin. *The Negro in the Civil War*. New York: Da Capo, 1989.

Quillen, Frank U. *The Color Line in Ohio: A History of Race Prejudice in a Typical Northern State*. New York: Negro Universities Press, 1969.

Rael, Patrick. *Black Identity & Black Protest in the Antebellum North*. Chapel Hill: University of North Carolina Press, 2002.

Ranck, George Washington. *History of Lexington, Kentucky: Its Early Annals and Recent Progress, Including Biographical Sketches and Personal Reminiscences of the Pioneer Settlers, Notices of Prominent Citizens, Etc., Etc.* Cincinnati: Robert Clarke, 1872.

Rankin, David C. "The Origins of Black Leadership in New Orleans during Reconstruction." *Journal of Southern History* 40, no. 3 (August 1974): 417–40.

Reed, Christopher Robert. *Black Chicago's First Century*. Vol. 1, *1833–1900*. Columbia: University of Missouri Press, 2005.

Rhodes, Jane. *Mary Ann Shadd Cary: The Black Press and Protest in the Nineteenth Century*. Bloomington: Indiana University Press, 1998.

Richardson, Heather Cox. *The Death of Reconstruction: Race, Labor, and Politics in the Post–Civil War North, 1865–1901*. Cambridge, MA: Harvard University Press, 2001.

Ripley, C Peter, ed. *The Black Abolitionist Papers*. Vol. 2, *Canada, 1830–1865*. Chapel Hill: University of North Carolina Press, 1986.

Robinson, Armstead. "Beyond the Realm of Social Consensus: New Meanings of Reconstruction for American History." *Journal of American History* 68, no. 2 (September 1981): 276–97.

Rodabaugh, James H. "The Negro in Ohio." *Journal of Negro History* 31, no. 1 (January 1946): 9–29.

Rollin, Frank A. *Life and Public Services of Martin R. Delany.* Boston: Lee and Shepard, 1883. Reprint, New York: Arno Press and the New York Times, 1969.

Saville, Julie. *The Work of Reconstruction: From Slave to Wage Laborer in South Carolina, 1860–1870.* Cambridge: Cambridge University Press, 1996.

Schwartzberg, Beverly. "'Lots of Them Did That': Desertion, Bigamy, and Marital Fluidity in Late-Nineteenth-Century America." *Journal of Social History* 37, no. 3 (Spring 2004): 573–600.

Schweninger, Loren. "Prosperous Blacks in the South, 1790–1880." *American Historical Review* 95, no. 1 (February 1990): 31–56.

Shelby, Tommie. "Two Conceptions of Black Nationalism: Martin Delany on the Meaning of Black Political Solidarity." *Political Theory* 31, no. 5 (October 2003): 664–92.

Siddali, Silvana. *From Property to Person: Slavery and the Confiscation Acts, 1861–1862.* Baton Rouge: Louisiana State University Press, 2005.

Siebert, Wilbur H. *The Underground Railroad from Slavery to Freedom.* New York: Macmillan, 1898. Reprint, New York: Arno Press and the New York Times, 1968.

Simeone, James. *Democracy and Slavery in Frontier Illinois: The Bottomland Republic.* DeKalb: Northern Illinois University Press, 2000.

Simmons, William. *Men of Mark.* Cleveland: George M. Rewell, 1887. Reprint, Chicago: Johnson, 1970.

Simon, Paul. *Freedom's Champion: Elijah Lovejoy.* Carbondale: Southern Illinois University Press, 1994.

Smith, J. Clay, Jr. *Emancipation: The Making of the Black Lawyer, 1844–1944.* Philadelphia: University of Pennsylvania Press, 1993.

Stafford, Hanford Dozier. "Slavery in a Border City: Louisville, 1790–1860." PhD diss., University of Kentucky, 1982.

Staples, Thomas S. *Reconstruction in Arkansas, 1862–1874.* New York: Columbia University, 1923.

Steckel, Richard H. "Migration and Political Conflict: Precincts in the Midwest on the Eve of the Civil War." *Journal of Interdisciplinary History* 28, no. 4 (Spring 1998): 583–603.

Stetson, Charlotte. *Alton, Illinois: A Pictorial History.* St. Louis: G. Bradley, 1968.

St. Hilaire, Joseph M. "The Negro Delegates to the Arkansas Constitutional Convention of 1868: A Group Profile." *Arkansas Historical Quarterly* 33, no. 1 (Spring 1974): 38–69.

Still, William. *Still's Underground Rail Road Records.* Philadelphia: William Still, Publisher, 1886.

Swain, Carol M. *Black Faces, Black Interests: The Representation of African Americans in Congress.* Cambridge, MA: Harvard University Press, 1993.

Taft, George S. *Compilation of Senate Election Cases from 1789 to 1885.* Washington, DC: Government Printing Office, 1885.

Tallant, Harold D. *Evil Necessity: Slavery and Political Culture in Antebellum Kentucky.* Lexington: University Press of Kentucky, 2003.

Taylor, Alrutheus Ambush. "Historians of the Reconstruction." *Journal of Negro History* 23, no. 1 (January 1938): 16–34.

———. *The Negro in the Reconstruction of Virginia.* Washington, DC: Association for the Study of Negro Life and History, 1926.

———. *The Negro in South Carolina during the Reconstruction.* Washington, DC: Association for the Study of Negro Life and History, 1924.

Taylor, Nikki. "Reconsidering the 'Forced' Exodus of 1829: Free Black Emigration from Cincinnati, Ohio to Wilberforce, Canada." *Journal of African American History* 87, no. 3 (Summer 2002): 283–302.

Toplin, Robert Brent. "Between Black and White: Attitudes toward Southern Mulattoes, 1830–1861." *Journal of Southern History* 45, no. 2 (May 1979): 185–200.

Townsend, William H. *Lincoln and the Bluegrass: Slavery and Civil War in Kentucky.* Lexington: University of Kentucky Press, 1955.

Trelease, Allen W. "Republican Reconstruction in North Carolina: A Roll-Call Analysis of the State House of Representatives, 1868–1870." *Journal of Southern History* 42, no. 3 (August 1976): 319–44.

Trotter, Joe William, Jr. *River Jordan: African American Urban Life in the Ohio Valley.* Lexington: University Press of Kentucky, 1998.

Trudeau, Noah Andre. *Black Troops in the Civil War, 1862–1865.* Boston: Little, Brown, 1998.

Twain, Mark. *Life on the Mississippi.* New York: Signet Classic, 2001.

Ullman, Victor. *Martin R. Delany: The Beginnings of Black Nationalism.* Boston: Beacon, 1971.

Vincent, Stephen A. *Southern Seed, Northern Soil: African-American Farm Communities in the Midwest, 1765–1900.* Bloomington: Indiana University Press, 1999.

Voegeli, V. Jacque. *Free but Not Equal: The Midwest and the Negro during the Civil War.* Chicago: University of Chicago Press, 1967.

Wade, Richard. *Slavery in the Cities: The South, 1820–1860.* London: Oxford University Press, 1964.

Waldrep, Christopher. *Roots of Disorder: Race and Criminal Justice in the American South, 1817–1880.* Urbana: University of Illinois Press, 1998.

Walker, Juliet E. K. *Free Frank: A Black Pioneer on the Antebellum Frontier.* Lexington: University Press of Kentucky, 1983.

———. *The History of Black Business in America: Capitalism, Race, Entrepreneurship.* New York: Macmillan Library Reference, 1998.

Way, Frederick, Jr. "Mississippi Scene." *S & D Reflector* 12, no. 3 (September 1975): 40–46.

———. *Way's Packet Directory, 1848–1983: Passenger Steamboats of the Mississippi River System since the Advent of Photography in Mid-continent America.* Athens: Ohio University Press, 1983.

Webb, Benedict Joseph. *The Centenary of Catholicity in Kentucky.* Louisville: C. A. Rogers, 1884.

Whayne, Jeannie M., ed. *Shadows over Sunnyside: An Arkansas Plantation in Transition, 1830–1945.* Fayetteville: University of Arkansas Press, 1993.

Wilkie, Jane Riblett. "Urbanization and De-urbanization of the Black Population before the Civil War." *Demography* 13, no. 3 (August 1976): 311–28.

Wilson, William Julius. *The Declining Significance of Race: Blacks and Changing American Institutions.* Chicago: University of Chicago Press, 1978.

Winkle, Kenneth J. *The Politics of Community: Migration and Politics in Antebellum Ohio.* Cambridge: Cambridge University Press, 1988.

Wintory, Blake. "William Hines Furbush: African-American Carpetbagger, Republican, Fusionist, and Democrat." *Arkansas Historical Quarterly* 63, no. 2 (Summer 2004): 107–65.

Woodward, C. Vann. *The Strange Career of Jim Crow.* New York: Oxford University Press, 2002.

Woodward, Earl F. "The Brooks and Baxter War in Arkansas, 1872–1874." *Arkansas Historical Quarterly* 30, no. 4 (Winter 1971): 315–36.

Wright, John D., Jr. *Lexington: Heart of the Bluegrass.* Lexington, KY: Lexington–Fayette County Historic Preservation Commission, 1982.

Yater, George H. *Two Hundred Years at the Falls of the Ohio: A History of Louisville and Jefferson County.* 2nd ed. Louisville: Filson Club, 1987.

Young, R. J. *Antebellum Black Activists: Race, Gender, and Self.* New York: Garland, 1996.

Zucker, Charles N. "The Free Negro Question: Race Relations in Ante-bellum Illinois, 1801–1860." PhD diss., Northwestern University, 1972.

Index

Reynolds, Susan, 31
Richardson, Cyrus "C. C.," 43, 44, 45, 112
Roberts, Peter, 21
Robinson, John, 45
Robinson, Rev. R. J., 43, 44, 112

Saunders, John H., 100
Schwartzberg, Beverly, 35, 37
Searle, E. J., 99, 113
Shadd, Abram W., 102, 103, 111
Shadd, Mary Ann, 28. *See also* Cary, Mary Ann Shadd
Shirley, Zack, 16
Simmons, William, 6
slaves: and James Barbour family, 10–11; contacts with free blacks in Louisville, 15–16; Cornelia's experience as, 9; in Lexington, 7–8; and Ratels, 9
Smith, Volney V., 77–78
Snyder, Oliver P., 81
Spradling, Washington, 14, 19, 112
steamboats, 14, 15; earnings on, 16; meals on, 57; and slavery, 16; stewards, 15, 16; and Underground Railroad, 16
Stewart, Maria, 38
St. Louis, Mo., 6, 15, 40, 46

Tankersley, Charles, 89
Taylor, A. A., 70
Tilly, Madison, 32
Torrans, James, 77, 81
True American, 20

Turner, James Milton, 54
Twain, Mark, 15
Twenty-Ninth United States Colored Infantry, 48, 50

Underground Railroad, 15, 16, 33, 43
Union Baptist Church (Alton), 43, 59
Union Depot, 56, 57, 75
Union Hotel, 56, 57, 59, 77

Vatble, Theophile Aristide, 8, 12, 17, 19, 113

Walker, Franklin P., 96–97, 99, 101, 102
Western Transit Insurance Company, 56, 78
White, Edwards "Dempy," 43, 54, 112
White, Jack, 105, 106
White, James T., 79, 93, 96
white middle class, 1
Wilkerson, Emmanuel, 43
Williams, Daniel Hale, 114
Willson, Joseph, 6
Wilson, William Julius, 2
Woodward, C. Vann, 108
Worthington, Elisha, 12, 92–93, 96
Wynn, Wathal, 100, 102, 103

Yates, Gov. Richard, 48, 54, 59, 83, 98, 113
Young, R. J., 24

VICTORIA L. HARRISON is an instructor in the Department of Historical Studies at Southern Illinois University Edwardsville. Her essays include "We Are Here Assembled: Illinois Colored Conventions, 1853–1873," published in the fall-winter 2015 issue of the *Journal of the Illinois State Historical Society*, and "Bastion or Bad Guy: Ngo Dinh Diem and the Press, 1957–1963," in the 2016 book *The Vietnam War in Popular Culture: The Influence of America's Most Controversial War on Everyday Life*, volume 1, edited by Ron Milam.